Great Kids

Great Kids

*Helping Your Baby and Child
Develop the Ten Essential Qualities for a
Happy, Healthy Life*

· · · · · · · · · · · ·

STANLEY I. GREENSPAN, M.D.

A MERLOYD LAWRENCE BOOK
DA CAPO PRESS
A Member of the Perseus Books Group

Copyright © 2007 by Stanley I. Greenspan, M.D.

Designed by Trish Wilkinson
Set in 12.5-point Adobe Garamond

First Da Capo Press edition 2007
ISBN-10 0-7382-0979-1
ISBN-13 978-0-7382-0979-1

A CIP data record for this book is available from the Library of Congress.

Published by Da Capo Press
A Member of the Perseus Books Group
www.dacapopress.com

Da Capo Press books are available at special discounts for bulk purchases in the U.S. by corporations, institutions, and other organizations. For more information, please contact the Special Markets Department at the Perseus Books Group, 2300 Chestnut Street, Suite 200, Philadelphia, PA, 19103, or call (800) 255-1514 or e-mail special.markets@perseusbooks.com.

1 2 3 4 5 6 7 8 9

Contents

··················

5

Emotional Range

Passion and Balance 87

6

Genuine Self-Esteem

The Importance of Self-Awareness 103

7

Internal Discipline

Perseverance and Self-Control 125

8

Creativity and Vision

A Rich Internal Life 147

9

Logical Thinking

Making Sense of the World 167

10

Moral Integrity

A Matter of the Heart 185

This book is dedicated to all the children of the world. They all have within them the potential to be great kids. It's our job to create a great world where this potential can flourish.

Preface

....

A lot is expected of children today. For many years, as a business-man, I've been interested in the kinds of competency needed for success in a rapidly changing world. As technology and modes of communication advance at warp speed, the traits needed in order to shape a full and successful life have also changed. Schools, companies, professional organizations, even professional sports teams, have come to realize that being "smart" or having great physical skill is not enough to succeed now in our world. The batteries of tests they give to prospective applicants try to uncover what lies "beneath," that is, what can we expect from this person above and beyond the usual? Savvy admissions directors and employers are looking for qualities such as emotional balance, logical thinking, discipline, ability to function under pressure, self-confidence, the ability to lead, etc. They've learned from their own past experience that these qualities are, if anything, more imperative for success than specific talents or "brains."

Thirty years ago, when I looked into this question of essential traits, I was fortunate to learn about a group of professionals in early child development who were meeting regularly to share their research into the most basic needs of children and how parents can meet them. Among these forward-thinking individuals were Reginald Lourie, T. Berry Brazelton, Stanley Greenspan, Selma Freiberg, Albert Solnit, Sally Provence, Ron Lally, Julius Richmond, Peter Neubauer, Leon Yarrow, and Robert Nover. I was invited to participate and, after just one meeting, it was clear to me that we had a golden opportunity to do something meaningful for kids. This group welcomed the help of a businessman and together we created an organization devoted to helping families raise socially, emotionally, and cognitively healthy children. Thus, Zero to Three was born.

Today we have a multidisciplinary board of thirty-five experts in various fields and a marvelous and talented staff of more than seventy-five executing a budget approaching fifteen million dollars annually. Our goal is to give parents the information and support they need to do the best job possible. Although love is the most important ingredient in a parent-child relationship, it is just not enough. As parents, we must be informed if we want our kids to go out confidently into the world, to be happy and successful. I learned in business that it was more important to work smart than to work hard. Being a great parent today means being a smart parent.

In witnessing the impressive work of each of the brilliant clinicians in our organization, I was particularly drawn to the ideas of Stanley Greenspan, especially to his practice with developmentally challenged children. Instead of limiting therapy to behavioral training and the rote learning of simple tasks, he works to get inside the psyche of his patients. The result is not only a more cognitively accomplished child but a warm child with a healthy full range of emotions. Some of these kids bore a diagnosis of autism or speech delay, which turned out to be wrong. I have seen this with my own eyes. After twenty years of witnessing these minor (major to the parents) miracles, it occurred to me that if Stanley Greenspan could accomplish this with challenged children, we could apply this knowledge to help all our kids become richer in qualities that are paramount in life.

How to identify universally valuable qualities described in this book? We first compiled a broad list. We then needed to cull this list and get consensus on qualities that most of us would agree are critical to success in life. The traits selected were ones that child development experts, parents, and business leaders all valued as qualities important for kids to develop in order to become healthy, successful adults. It was important that parents value these traits so that they would want to encourage them. It was important that child development experts agree on the characteristics that are valuable not only in childhood but also for the later challenges that come with adolescence, marriage, career, parenthood. It was important to satisfy the various professional people we polled who knew very well what qualities were most important for success in their fields. With that first long list, we then asked a great range of people to choose the "must have" qualities, and to rank them. This group, spread across the United States and Canada, included professionals in medicine, law, the arts, education, and executives from all kinds of organizations. All had experience seeing how some people succeeded and some failed, and why. Spouses or partners answered independently. Bringing my own preconceived notions to the table, I was sure that men would rank the qualities differently than women, and that businessmen would have a different take than educators. People in the technical fields would respond differently than those in the arts. We all assumed that easterners see things differently than westerners or those in the Midwest. We also assumed that the various cultural groups would respond differently. Wrong in every case! People responded completely as individuals and came up with a set of nearly universally valued qualities. There was agreement across gender, professions, and cultures.

Irving Harris, a board member, my idol as a philanthropist, and a very astute thinker, had suggested that we add "inquisitiveness" to the broad list. Our respondents confirmed this, usually under the label "curiosity." A social scientist might say that this list reflects the values of upscale America. It is true that the people polled were successful in their careers, not necessarily wealthy, but successful. However, their backgrounds differed greatly. Looking at the challenges facing a child in the early twenty-first century (the only way we can make a judgment), these qualities struck our respondents and ourselves as being essential. One would be very right in saying that there are other important qualities, but a child equipped with the ten described here would have a major head start in life.

The good news in this book is that parents can encourage the development of qualities in their children that many wise people think are vital for a full and accomplished life. In short, they can "raise the bar" for their kids. Encouraging these important traits requires a lot of competence in parents as well. Recognizing the new expectations facing children today, many parents are searching for just the kind of clear guidance offered in this book.

As you will see, the focus is not on IQ or great talent. Success in life and career depends on multiple abilities. The qualities you will read about here, such as emotional balance, logical thinking, internal discipline, self-awareness, and empathy, are the foundations without which brilliant intelligence and talents may flounder.

Globalization, environmental threats, new technologies, and political conflict will challenge the next generation worldwide. In this smaller and flatter world, the most important thing that we can do is give our kids the qualities needed to survive and thrive.

Bernard Levy
Co-Director, Infant Development Specialist Program
Floortime Foundation™

Acknowledgments

....

I would like to thank Sarah Mahoney, who made essential contributions to this work. Her gifted illustrative examples and lively writing style are reflected in the spirit and content of *Great Kids*. I also want to thank Nancy Breslau Lewis for her vital help in the writing of some of the sections of this work. I'd also like to express my appreciation to Sue Morrisson for her administrative support, to Sarah Miller for the many ways in which she helps the families we work with, and to Jan Tunney who also provided administrative support in the early stages of this book.

I can't express enough appreciation to Merloyd Lawrence who brings a sensitivity and organization in the way she edits. She has made the book *Great Kids* live up to the characteristics that we find in great kids.

Introduction
Growing Great Kids

....

You know who they are. They're the fourth-grade boys who dash out to be first to greet their teacher and help her unload her car. They're the sixteen-year-old girls who invite a new classmate to sit with them at lunch. They're the toddlers who take turns and shout with glee at the slide, and the infants who gaze lovingly into their mothers' eyes.

They're great kids. How many times have you said, "That Josh is a great kid" or "I like my daughter's soccer teammates. They're great kids." We hear the phrase often, and we know what we mean when we say it. We're not talking about kids who get 1600s on their combined SATs or tennis champions or music prodigies—although of course those kids, too, can be great kids. We're talking about the lively, independent, friendly, and optimistic young people so many of us are lucky to know. Despite all the bad news about children today that seems to clog the airwaves, anyone who lives or works with kids knows that there's good news, too.

s" are emotionally and intellectually healthy people.

't refer to a specific temperamental quality, such as ~⊔ɪⅆness; nor does it depend on athletic skills or on musical or mathematical or artistic talent. Great kids come in all varieties. And, given the right nurturing and encouragement, all kids can be great kids.

Emotional and intellectual health involves some fundamental abilities and traits that underlie the skills and talents children may eventually develop. These abilities and traits have to do with how children (and adults) relate to one another and to the outside world. They begin to form in infancy and make possible the pursuit of success, wisdom, and rich relationships at every stage of life.

Engagement and empathy, for instance, begin with the first parent/infant exchanges and continue to fuel our understanding of, and caring for, the community and world we live in. Curiosity and logical thinking are the foundations of any kind of academic study, innovation, and organizational leadership. And without building the crucial abilities of self-awareness, emotional balance, and discipline, the potential of even the most gifted child will be at risk.

These qualities, and others that I'll describe in this book, are the source of children's future achievements and happiness. As we shall see, they all take root in early emotional experience, and parents can do a lot to offer such experience. Whatever children's degree of physical, intellectual, or artistic talent, these qualities expand the possibilities for their future.

The ten crucial traits described here comprise a child's intellectual and mental health. When all ten are present and fully functioning in a child, that's when we're likely to hear parents and other adults say, "Alicia (or Andy) is such a great kid." In fact, when we hear an adult described as "a great person," it's almost certainly because these ten skills are there.

Perhaps the most important point about these traits is that they are not wired in our genes—we aren't born with them. They come from experience, which means that each and every child—even those with challenges—can strive to acquire them, with the help of caring adults. In this book, I'll unbraid the strands of great kids' intellectual, emotional, and social selves to find out how these traits develop. We will see in detail the kinds of nurturing that encourage each trait. We will also see how emotional and intellectual development are dynamically intertwined throughout a child's development.

What do most parents want for their children? I believe there are three essentials: Parents want their children to have happy and fulfilled lives, raise healthy families of their own, and contribute to society in a meaningful way. The characteristics of great kids identified here represent the skills needed to accomplish each of these goals. It's a long journey from infancy through toddlerhood and the early school years, then on through adolescence to the cusp of adulthood. A "great kid" moves through identifiable intellectual and emotional landscapes and past important landmarks along the way.

With each step toward selfhood, children learn new cognitive skills. As we shall see, these are built upon their emotional experiences. As they grow, children move through the full range of emotions—joy, sadness, anger, love, triumph, and loss. The traits that we describe grow through such emotional experiences and along clear developmental stages.

Before I begin, let's look at the developmental roadmap that I'll be referring to in each chapter as I discuss the ten characteristics of "great kids" in detail. A child must reach certain landmarks on the road to adulthood. We all traveled this road; now our children are embarking on it. Before we look closely at the specific pathways to empathy and curiosity and emotional balance and all the other characteristics, let's look at the stages through which they will develop.

Awakening to the World.   Beginning at birth, we learn how to be calm and regulated and to take an interest in the world and all its sensations of touch, sound, smell, and taste.

Engaging and Relating.   As we become part of relationships with our parents and caregivers and the others who love us, we, in turn, fall in love with the world.

Communicating.   The long process of learning how to communicate with those we love starts with the simplest of purposeful gestures: smiles, head nods, frowns, angry grimaces, deliberate pointing. Most important, we learn how to respond to our caregivers' gestures with gestures of our own.

Problem Solving and a Sense of Self.   Long before we learn to use words to any degree, we learn to use gestures to solve problems. We figure out that we can take a parent by the hand and walk to the toy or cookie that we want. We make gurgling sounds to show that it's this one, not that one, as the parent questions us about our preference. This continuous flow of gesturing with others helps us use our senses of hearing, vision, touch, and movement as a well-orchestrated team. We feel ourselves acting on the world and, through social interactions, we learn about our parents' values and the norms of our culture. All this happens before we can speak.

Language and Ideas.   Now, we learn to connect and use emotional ideas. They guide our pretend play. Words now make it possible for us to let others know how we feel and what we want them to do for us.

Logic.   Once we learn to share our ideas, we take another huge leap and begin to build bridges between them. We begin to think logically. We can explain why we're happy or sad. We also learn to refrain from something not just because we'll be punished for it but because it's "wrong." Our feelings about ourselves begin to be based on our own evaluation of whether we've done the right or wrong thing.

Once we've crossed into the world of logical thinking and connecting our emotions and ideas together, we can master higher and higher levels of emotional and intellectual development. As we grow into adulthood, we move through other predictable stages, more sophisticated kinds of thinking, and self-reflection.

In this journey that we all make, we will see how the key traits that we've identified continue to expand and enhance the lives of great kids. By nurturing them, we can help our children build close relationships, productive careers, strong families, and a deepening sense of the meaning they choose to give to their lives.

1

Engagement
Relating to Others

....

I visited a new mother, a friend of the family, in the hospital recently. When I entered her room, she was holding her infant in the crook of one arm and using her free hand to pack a small suitcase for the trip home. The baby was awake and alert, looking out from the safety of her mother's arm, smelling her, and feeling her warmth. As my friend packed, she crooned a bit to her new daughter. This connection, only hours old, was off to a good start. Mom was relaxed and enjoying her contact with her new daughter; the baby was warm, secure, nestled into loving arms. A relationship was beginning.

The lessons of engagement begin with the intimacy of a baby's bonds with her parents. As this little girl grows older, she will form strong bonds with all her immediate family by learning to trust, to communicate, and to work and play together. In her relations with others, she will learn about frustration and anger, about disappointment and sadness. As she grows, she will move away from the immediacy of her family circle into a world of peers and, later, into larger groups. Learning how to engage and take pleasure in other people—from elementary school friends to high school buddies to teachers, boyfriends, a husband, and eventually her own children—begins from the moment she first looks into her mother's eyes and takes pleasure in her mother's closeness.

The ability to engage with another person is the bedrock skill for the development of a great kid. From it grows her ability to form trusting relationships. Through relationships, a child learns to construct not only a sense of self but also of the reality of the world in which she lives.

Throughout her life, a child must be able to "read" and relate to a range of people. As she grows up, this ability to connect will allow her to make friends and form a variety of relationships with significant loved ones, with casual acquaintances, and with colleagues and clients. In times of stress, she will turn to those close to her to help her feel better and to find solutions to problems. Through connection with others, children and adults share the pleasures, joys, angers, and sorrows of their lives.

HOW ENGAGEMENT BEGINS

As we can see in the scene I witnessed at the hospital, connection begins immediately. The capacity to elicit connection develops quickly, as well. By the time she is four months old, my friend's baby will be wooing her mother with winning smiles—and getting smiles in return. The pleasure of this reciprocity builds her trust in relationships and her sense of her own ability to connect with other people. By the time she's eight months old, she will be flirting with caregivers, and even with strangers; she will actively be playing peek-a-boo, laughing, and reaching out.

Relating Through Joy

During the first few months of life, babies learn to translate the world of their sensations into emotions. They begin to understand that a world exists outside themselves, represented at first by Daddy's face, Mommy's smell, the comfort of a soft blanket, the shock of a banging door or a loud voice. Recognizing these patterns and learning the difference between "me" and "outside me" is an essential step toward connecting with a reality outside themselves.

At the very beginning, that reality is grounded in a continuous set of sensations: temperature, touch, taste, hearing, smell, and the sight of familiar faces. The baby I saw in the hospital was already using all her senses, and those senses were focused on the presence of her mother—as they were on her father, too, when he held her in his arms. As parents nuzzle and croon, feed and bathe, cuddle and soothe their baby, their engagement with their infant brings her intense pleasure. This interaction gives the baby her first emotional experience. Through those feelings, she will quickly learn essential lessons about the outer world and about how human beings function in it.

D. W. Winnicott, the great British psychoanalyst, offers a delightfully vivid account of this early engagement:

> There is the reactive smile that means little or nothing but there is also the smile that eventually turns up that means that the infant feels loving, and feels loving at that moment towards the mother. Later, the infant splashes her in the bath or pulls her hair or bites the lobes of her ear or gives her a hug, and all that sort of thing. . . . On account of this, the infant is able to make a new development and integration.

It's easy to take the human ability to connect for granted. After all, we all have parents, many of us have siblings, and we all operate in a world filled with other human beings. But this ability to connect varies a great deal. Some children need to sneak away to play alone in their own rooms when they're upset. Others escape into video games, computers, or the television—essentially isolated activities. Others seek to establish connection by fighting, behaving provocatively, or irritating others to force attention.

Parents take great joy in the period of their baby's life when she begins to respond with coos of pleasure and bursts of laughter to interactive games. Mommy might put a rattle on top of her head to make the infant laugh, and then repeat the game. This funny exchange reinforces the baby's understanding that Mommy is a person separate from her. It also teaches the baby that by responding to silly games with laughter and smiles, she can keep the connection going.

Relating in Action: Solving Problems

As a toddler, a little girl might lead a parent by the hand to her playroom; then, through many gestures exchanged with a parent working as her partner, the toddler is able to communicate that she wants a specific toy. "No, I want the red truck, not the blue bunny," she might as well be saying, although she does not use words yet. These "conversations" with sounds and gestures that go on between babies and parents or other close caregivers serve to cement the bonds between them.

At a Mother's Day picnic, two toddlers who see each other fairly often were playing with a red wagon. Meg sat in the wagon, and Will tried to pull her along. The yard was scattered with toys— a large plastic dump truck, a half-deflated empty wading pool, and a pile of hula-hoops belonging to Meg's four-and-a-half-year-old sister. As the adults sat in a circle enjoying the spring day and each other's company, I watched as the two children took on their important project: moving the red wagon.

Will gave his job of pulling the wagon all his strength. As he grunted and groaned, the wagon inched forward right into the pile of hula-hoops, where it got stuck again. From her perch in the wagon Meg gestured emphatically at the hoops: "Get those darned things out of the way," she seemed to be saying. Will got the message immediately. He carefully picked up each hoop and moved it aside. Meg climbed out and helped him. When the way was clear, and after a little gentle tussling over whose turn it was to sit in the wagon and whose turn it was to pull (Meg won), they tried again. This time, the wagon rolled slowly forward as the little boy pulled. He laughed triumphantly and ran over to his mother for the reward of a quick hug. Once their problem was solved, the toddlers traded places and Meg pulled for a while. But they quickly lost interest in the wagon and turned instead to the fascinating matter of watching their older brother and sister use the garden hose to fill the wading pool.

This little scene demonstrates something essential in a child's burgeoning ability to connect with another person—this time a peer. At ten months, Will and Meg enjoyed looking over toys together, but they didn't interact much. By eighteen months, they were more interested in each other, giving each other hugs and pats when they met, mussing each other's hair, and checking out each other's toy-of-the-day. Now, at two-and-a-half, they take on roles in their play (I sit, you pull) and work together as they clear the way for a wagon ride.

When you watch your toddler with playmates you are likely to see this shared social problem solving in action. Toddlers will giggle together, take turns, and clearly show affection for each other—and often a preference for one playmate over another. You can see a clear communication system beginning—even before they speak to each other in sentences. As the children grow older, their play will evolve into shared, pretend games that also involve using words.

At the picnic I described, the grown-ups wisely stayed out of Will and Meg's project. They were nearby in case they were needed (as they were later, when Meg fell and skinned her knee). They were there to mediate if gentle pushes escalated into angry shoves. But when the children were playing and having fun, these smart parents stayed out of their way. If, on the other hand, Meg and Will had stayed in parallel play, one of their parents could have encouraged them to team up by playing a simple game. Dad might hide and encourage the toddlers to find him, for example.

Watching this early relationship between toddler friends, we can see that by connecting with each other the children are also learning to manage a range of feelings—disappointment over the failure to move the wagon, jealousy over who sits and who pulls, triumph when a challenge is overcome. All these feelings are part of relationships and will continue to be so throughout life. As children learn to tolerate such feelings and balance assertiveness with cooperation, their relationships become broader and more stable, less easily disrupted by conflict or frustration.

Relating in Imaginative Play

In the preschool years, pretend play is a big part of relating. Zachary and Annie don't attend the same school, but they often play together in their neighborhood. They're good friends and show a marked preference for spending time together. Their parents often hear them talking as they make up stories for Annie's stuffed tigers and lions. They often stage a "dinner party." (Annie's parents frequently entertain at home.) Each child assumes voices for the animals as they slurp imaginary soup and eat imaginary cupcakes. After a while, usually at Zachary's insistence, the toy animals revert to their wild state and the children pretend they are in a jungle. The play is accompanied by hair-raising roars and howls.

Annie and Zachary's imaginative play, deeply satisfying to them both, is not without conflict. A bit more assertive than his friend, Zachary sometimes goes over the line with physical boisterousness, and Annie pulls back from their game. Nevertheless, they are making important strides in their developing relationships. Their play has become more complex and now involves language and ideas. They are learning to take turns, to express preferences, and to explain themselves. Their friendship is characterized by a warmth and intimacy that prefigures the close friendships they will have with their peers as they grow up. As a pair, they are working together to learn more about how to connect. Soon, they will enter a world of school in which more complex patterns in pairs, trios, and groups operate. They are well on their way to having the skills to negotiate that world.

As a child's relationships move through these developmental stages, it's important to remember that not all children go through them at the same pace. Each stage emerges in its own way, and each stage offers another opportunity to play out previous stages, including missed opportunities for connection, whether it's with parents, caregivers, or other children.

Relating in Triangles

For their joint birthdays, preschooler Nathan's mom and dad went away for a long weekend together, leaving their son with his grandmother. He had fun playing in the pool, visiting the zoo, and helping out in the garden. He rarely asked where Mommy and Daddy were. He knew they were on a trip and that they would be back in three days.

When the big moment arrived, Nathan ran to the door to greet his parents: "Daddy, daddy, I love you!" he shouted, leaping into his father's arms. He didn't say a word to Mommy, although he gave her a quick hug. Mommy, already tired from the plane flight home, burst into tears. Nathan may have meant to hurt his mother a little for going off and leaving him, but he quickly went over to her to make her feel better.

This little boy is beginning to discover his power within the triangle of his family, learning that he can have an influence over the complex, give-and-take relationship that exists among three people. Of course, Nathan loves Mommy, too, and she knows it. But they are both finding out that even a four-year-old has the power to hurt someone's feelings.

At his preschool, Nathan is also learning the effects of his behavior. Usually he figures out how to smoothly enter a game that two other children have begun, perhaps by volunteering a toy or simply by sitting beside them until he becomes integrated into their sandbox project or truck race. But sometimes he barges in and knocks over the blocks; when he does this, the other boys turn away from him. In his enthusiasm and haste to join in, he misses signals that his approach isn't working. When Nathan's teacher notices that some of the other children are excluding him, she tries to help him modify his rambunctious and aggressive approach. At home, his parents have begun inviting a couple of neighbors' kids over for an informal play group to help their son learn how to operate when more than two people are involved.

By acquiring the skill to gauge other's reactions to him and so modify his behavior accordingly (or not, if he feels like making trouble), Nathan is working on social skills that he will need for the rest of his life. How well he learns to interpret and follow the rules, or bend them when necessary for his own desires, will affect his relationships for years to come.

Relating in Peer Groups

By the third or fourth grade, peer relationships have become increasingly challenging for them. Playground politics becomes the order of the day. This is where a child's multiple relationships really blossom and she becomes a social being. At this age, planning and gathering in groups occupy a huge amount of children's time and thought. Also of profound interest is where everyone ranks within the group, a hierarchy that changes from day to day, seemingly from moment to moment.

Ask a child embroiled in playground politics who's in or who's out, who's up or who's down, and she will know. Children will rank-order their own friends into best and second best and so on—and these rankings keep shifting. Keeping track of everyone's status is a full-time job.

Watch the playground at any elementary school and you will see groups in action. Knots of girls gather in circles, their backs to the rest of the children. They whisper and laugh and plan. And someone, inevitably, is left outside.

Alexa, a shy and sensitive girl, dreads recess because she knows that most of the other girls will gather together and leave her on her own. Alexa's seeming inability to connect with her peers on the playground doesn't mean that she is socially inept in all situations, however. Children, like adults, show a wide range of relating styles. Alexa is skilled and sensitive when one-on-one with another child, or even in threesomes of friends. But she shrinks from larger gatherings. Who hasn't met an adult who feels overwhelmed by large gatherings and avoids the office holiday party, grade-level parent meetings at school, and other large-group events?

Armed with a friend, Katie, Alexa can venture with confidence onto the playground and find things to do at recess. Slowly, she and Katie may even integrate into the larger, more chaotic groups that some children find so easy to manage. With the support and understanding of her parents and her teacher, Alexa can begin to understand that she is a little shy. She's beginning to learn that she can trust her close friend to hold her hand and shore her up when she feels hesitant. Learning about one's own style of interacting is an important step on the road to navigating the groups that are inevitable at school, at work, and at play, whether it's a middle-school dance or an opening-of-school cookout attended by a hundred families.

During the grade school years, kids move into a more complex social world. They learn to interpret others' positions and to balance their own positions with the group. They begin to see relationships in shades of gray rather than in stark black and white. For example, Gillian came home from school and announced to her mother that Heather was no longer her second-best friend. "What happened?" her mother asked. "I thought you two were practically inseparable."

"She sat with the mean girls at lunch," Gillian said. "And there wasn't even room for me. She likes them more than she likes me. But I don't care because Alice likes me better than she likes Heather. She sat with me even though the mean girls asked her to sit at their table."

The lunchroom and playground drama of grade school is so consuming for children that it's remarkable they get any work done. As they watch their children ride the waves of conflict created by middle-school social upheaval, parents can feel challenged. It helps to remember that these negotiations, as petty and painful as they seem, are helping children figure out who they are. Most grade-school children will follow the pressures of the group for a while before they have the confidence and maturity to strike out on their own into the more internally focused territory of adolescence.

Negotiating within and among groups allows new social skills to emerge. By enduring teasing and exclusion, and by finding ways to deal with them, kids find ways to coexist effectively and happily with others.

Adolescent Relationships

A central task for the adolescent is the ability to form intimate relationships with others. Teenagers seek friendships that are closer than those they had before; these relationships have a more reflective and self-revealing tone than the connections made in grade school. When adolescents connect with peers, they build on their earlier experiences with intimacy and engagement in the family. These friendships can be intense and consuming. An adolescent may often tell her parents that only her friends "really understand me." Although it can be painful for parents when their kids turn away from them to forge close bonds with friends outside the family group, this is an important step forward for adolescents because they are becoming more and more aware that in the future they will be out in the world on their own. Intense, one-on-one intimacy is hard to maintain, however, and a teenager's close relationships ebb and flow during these years.

As grade schoolers move into adolescence, they must learn to balance the world inside themselves with the demands of school and family and community that they encounter every day. That external world begins to expand rapidly, and with that expansion come challenges about exploring sexuality and making decisions about risk-taking behaviors such as trying drugs and alcohol. They move into a world in which they must make multiple decisions based on their own internal standards. These standards were founded on their relationships with parents; later, they were polished and honed by the give-and-take of social life in grade school. In grade school, a child's sense of self is broadly drawn by what others think of her. In adolescence, independent of family and friends, she begins to reflect on herself and to understand who she is and what her values and beliefs are. These internal standards will shape her relationships.

In middle school, Jake was popular and sought after. A good athlete, attractive, and funny, he was at the center of his school's group of cool kids. But inwardly, Jake began longing to connect more closely. In high school, he found that relationship with a serious girlfriend. Together, they discussed politics and religion. They took long walks and made plans for the ways they would change the world. Becoming closer, they saw themselves as two sensitive idealists against the world.

Although some of Jake's friends were mystified by the change, Jake was making a good, and predictable, move: Having established comfort in relating to groups, he was now ready to examine his internal standards and more intensely test his sense of self. With his girlfriend, he explored ideas, articulated his ideals, and strengthened a sense of his own uniqueness.

Making this transition is not easy, and adolescents do it at different paces. Ready for a more mature relationship with his first love, Jake leaves some of his old friends in the dust. They, in turn, are baffled and feel betrayed by his defection. Jake needs to develop skills to negotiate the different levels of feeling and connection that different relationships require. As he does so, he will see similarities and differences between himself, his friends, his girlfriend, and his family, all of which bolster his sense of who he really is. Adulthood is close, and Jake is integrating the skills he needs to cross that bridge.

HELPING YOUR CHILD
ENGAGE WITH OTHERS

Your child's most fundamental need, after food and basic good health, is to engage with other people. Most infants do this effortlessly after the first weeks of life if their nervous or muscular systems aren't compromised in grievous ways and if they are embraced by loving caregivers. But we all respond to sights, sounds, touches, and movements with varying degrees of enthusiasm, and sometimes it takes a little effort to adjust your instinctive way of relating to your baby to the style that most easily engages her attention.

Your child's relationship with you will expand when you follow her lead and interests, and then build on these in ways that expand her experiences and tolerance for frustration. We call these times together Floortime™ because the window into your child's emotional and intellectual world opens most easily when you enter into *her* orbit at *her* eye level and on *her* terms. Although these times will come with toddlers and schoolchildren when you're literally playing on the floor with them, Floortime occurs in other ways with infants and teens.

When it comes to engaging your three-month-old's attention, for example, there's no better place than in your arms. After many weeks of intimate, face-to-face interactions, your baby comes to rely on your ability to "read" her, to know how her nervous system works, and, most especially, how best to give her pleasure. Perhaps you've noticed a brightening in her eyes each time you widen your own eyes and raise your eyebrows when you gaze down at her, or how she seems to be more relaxed and less distracted by her flailing arms and legs when you wrap her snugly in a receiving blanket. Maybe you've observed that your baby's colicky cries ratchet down a notch when her daddy gently sways her to and fro and lulls her with a rhythmic, deep-pitched, "There, there, ba-by."

As you come to know your baby's likes and dislikes and adjust your own style to help her relax and enjoy herself, she learns that her smiles beget yours, and that engaging with you feels good. As the months pass, your baby's interest in relating to you will cause her to crane her neck up over the bumper pad in her crib when she hears you enter the room. You'll likely find yourself squatting down to meet her drooling smile with an ear-to-ear grin of your own. Your baby's interest in relating to you encourages her to turn to the source of her pleasure and stretch new muscles—which in turn wires new areas within her brain.

In this way, your baby's feelings begin playing a role very early in life by connecting what she sees or hears (sensations) with what she does (motor actions). At nine months, your baby's joy in engaging with you keeps growing as you exchange back-and-forth smiles, bobbing head nods, and silly squeaks. Such exchanges mark the beginning of what we call reciprocal communication; your child keeps investing in a world outside herself because it's so much fun. Games involving anticipation—such as "Peek-a-boo" and "How big is baby? S-o-o-o big!"—give particularly intense pleasure to a baby at this age. Your animated grinning and excited, high-pitched warbles magnify her joy each time you uncover her face or stretch her arms wide.

As your child grows, there will be many opportunities to help her enjoy relationships and build the skills of relating. For instance, with a toddler, parents can "play dumb" at times when she is thirsty and in search of a sippy cup or juice box. As she toddles to the kitchen, pointing to her mouth, for instance, don't rush to supply her with her heart's desire. To share her thigh-high view of the world, kneel down and point to the refrigerator with a quizzical look on your face. When she nods her head up and down, let her know by nodding in response that you've read her cue, that she's been understood, and that her desire will be fulfilled. This little "conversation" can go on. When you ask whether she'd like to have something to drink out of the refrigerator, wait until she delivers another nod or makes a sound before opening the door. Stand up and she'll likely stretch out her arms to be picked up, too. In this way you build on your child's interest and help her see how communicating with you is the key to her getting what she wants.

By the time a child is three or four, she can use words to express her desires and feelings. Now she will learn ways to remain in a warm relationship with you—even when she's distracted or sad or angry. Let's say she's had a tough day at preschool, or she's mad at you because you wouldn't let her wear her new shoes while she played under the sprinkler. She may literally give you the cold shoulder and turn her back to you while listlessly pushing a toy back and forth along the floor.

Even under these circumstances, you can follow your child's lead, enter into her world, and become a part of her interests. When these dues have been paid, your relationship is reinforced. You can help your child relate across a range of emotions; she will respond during frustrating as well as delightful times.

Say your child is banging a plastic horse angrily on the floor. Instead of telling her to stop, grab another toy horse and turn your leg into a hill; then casually say that only the mightiest and most powerful of all the horses can make it over that hill. It's usually only a matter of time before your little girl will have her horse galloping up your leg. As the little drama really gets cooking, you may get a few hints about the anger or disappointment your child has experienced earlier in the day. If her play involves a lot of stallions fighting in the corral and little else, you could try introducing a little subplot in which a colt is shunned by the others or is sent back to the corral by his mommy because he disobeyed her and fought with a smaller colt. Your child can learn to tolerate uncomfortable emotions within the cocoon of her relationship with you.

During the elementary school years, your child's ability to relate to her peers may become the focus of her life. Your shared activities with her can include your role-playing skills as she negotiates the Byzantine politics of the playground. She can practice with you as a "friend" or a player in whatever complex negotiations she is facing. Many children find it difficult to enter a social setting, or to take leave of a group, so practicing with Mom or Dad can help grease the skids into new relationships.

If your shy fourth grader desperately wants to play with some of the girls in her new class but hesitates to approach them for fear of being rejected, for example, you might look for a moment to suggest a sociable option that builds on a situation or skill that she's already comfortable with. If she's relaxed hanging out with her buddy next door, who's a friendly, welcoming child, you might propose that your daughter invite a new classmate over to ride bikes together with her old friend. Or if she's a whiz at bowling, suggest that she invite a new friend or two to join her; her feeling of physical mastery will help buoy her in the rougher waters of new relationships. The more opportunities your child has to play with others, the more comfortable she will become. It may be a time to bite your tongue and "happily" drive her and her friends back and forth to each other's houses.

A teenager's trials in forming relationships can be an intense roller coaster. She will rely on the strength of her relationship with you (despite repeated sighs that "you just don't get it") as she faces more intimate connections with friends outside your family group. Oddly enough, some of the most sustaining Floortime moments you'll share with your teenager will occur when you can't make direct eye contact, such as during phone conversations, for example, or long car rides in which the two of you sit next to each other, eyes locked on the road. As long as you continue to follow your teenager's conversational lead, just as you did during her toddler and school years, and give up the opportunity to preach, you'll find that the empathetic, familiar sound of your voice can be a powerful signal that you care and that she is understood.

Encouraging Engagement

1. Get to know how your child's nervous system works, her sensitivities and preferences.
2. Find out what brings her pleasure and where her interests lie.
3. Join her in her natural interests; follow her lead.
4. Explore your relationship by expanding the range of your activities together.
5. Gradually broaden her relationships beyond her parents to siblings, other relatives, peers of the same sex and opposite sex, and other types of adults.
6. Encourage her to build greater intimacy in her relationships by helping her not to withdraw when the emotional going gets rough.

Why have I begun our journey through the essential characteristics for becoming a "great kid," and thus a great adult, with the capacity to relate to others? Because it is the most important skill we have. The ability to trust and to love allows us to live connected and meaningful lives. The ability to connect deeply with others is the bedrock upon which we construct our lifelong, intimate partnerships; establish and maintain friendships; and forge families. When we raise children of our own, and hope that they in turn will become great kids, we will use these skills all over again and model them every day.

2

Empathy
The Ability to Care

....

Kim was in her late twenties when her elderly cat finally had to be put to sleep. Kim was devastated, but she soldiered on, going to work the next day at the magazine where she was a copy editor as if nothing had happened. But her officemate, Steph, noticed that Kim's usual cheerful face was sad, and that she didn't seem as engaged in her work.

"What's wrong? You seem upset," Steph said.

"No big deal," Kim shrugged. "It's just that I had to have my cat put to sleep yesterday. But I'm fine, really. It was time—and he was only a cat, after all."

Steph didn't press the point. But at lunch, she slipped out and bought Kim a sympathy card and propped it on her colleague's desk. When Kim saw it, she began to cry and told Steph how much the cat had meant to her. He had been with her through thick and thin, ever since high school, always there. "I feel like I've lost part of my childhood," she said.

Steph listened and said, "I know how you feel."

And she did.

Steph's authentic sensitivity, her small gesture with the card, and her warmth made Kim feel comforted, less isolated in her sorrow. Empathy—the ability to sincerely understand someone else's feelings—enabled Steph to help her saddened friend.

When Steph empathized with Kim's sadness over her pet, her questions and her emotional tone—the way she gazed at her friend, her posture, her quiet voice—all conveyed a sense that she was there in Kim's shoes with her. Yet, at the same time, Steph was able to retain some distance from Kim's feelings; she didn't leap in and add her own remembered grief over lost pets to Kim's burden.

We've all had the experience with a friend or a relative or a parent who overdoes the sympathy. Yes, they step into our shoes. But then they take over and live there! That's not empathy.

We also have all known individuals who listen mechanically to our sorrow or our joy, and may even ask a few correct questions about it. Yet we can sense that they are just going through the motions; they don't really understand or really care about what we are saying. They're trying; they know intellectually that they *should* be empathetic. But they don't quite understand it at the feeling level, as Steph did.

How do we recognize true empathy? Truly empathetic people not only understand, and can almost rephrase, what you are saying and thinking, but also resonate with you emotionally. Their voices resonate with the way you feel. Their eyes resonate with the way you feel. Yet they maintain enough of their own sense of self to give you the space to breathe and experience your own feelings. They can comfort and soothe without intruding and taking over. They hit the right note of warm, empathetic concern.

Empathy is one of the most important characteristics of a great kid. Although some degree of empathy has been seen in babies (who cry, for instance, when another infant gets hurt, and even in some animals), *only the right kind of learning experiences bring out this empathy*—a skill that literally makes the world a better place.

THE ROOTS OF EMPATHY

It's two in the morning, and Timothy, three months old, is screaming at the top of his lungs. His mom tries feeding him, but he's crying too hard and too loud to nurse. His parents aren't sure what's wrong, but they can tell this baby is angry! His father takes his son out of his crib and sits in the rocker. The lights are on low. Dad sits with the baby and rocks him. "I know, I know," he says. "I know you're upset; I know you're feeling scared and uncomfortable. I know, I know." He rocks his son to the rhythm of his cries. Gradually, Tim calms down. Gradually, he feels safe and warm and loved. He and his father smile at each other and gurgle a little, back and forth. Finally, Tim falls asleep.

What does this nursery scene have to do with empathy? With a small baby, the first lessons in this trait come from those early warm relationships, from comfort when it is needed. Connecting with a caregiver helps a baby become a part of the human world not only by looking, listening, and attending to it but also by learning to expect warmth and love from familiar caregivers. This trust comes most often with the primary caregiver—mother, father, grandparent, or nanny—who is consistently loving, devoted, and warm.

Why does empathy begin here? Because without this primary nurturing relationship, a baby doesn't have reason to begin caring for other human beings. Those first cuddles and hugs are the port of entry for real caring and devotion. The depth of that warmth and the depth of that love become the depth of the love that the growing child carries in his heart, which in turn becomes the depth of his empathy for other people's sorrows and joys. A child will grow only as much empathy as was shown to him.

D. W. Winnicott caught these very early beginnings of empathy in *The Child, the Family, and the Outside World:*

> The pleasure the mother takes in what she does for the infant very quickly lets the infant know that there is a human being behind what is done. But what eventually makes the baby feel the person in the mother is perhaps the mother's special ability to put herself in the place of the infant, and so to know what the baby is feeling like. No book rules can take the place of this feeling a mother has for her infant's needs.

He goes on to say that "[t]he fact that the mother is able to make such delicate adaptation shows that she is a human being and the baby is not long in appreciating that fact."

In that primary relationship a baby experiences empathy for the first time when he is upset and his mom or dad or other caregiver rocks him in a rhythm that matches his feelings, as Tim's dad did. The adult resonates with the baby's screeching hunger, with his rage. At other times, the grown-up will also resonate with the baby's joy and excitement. The baby feels that resonance through the way Daddy rocks him, the way he looks at him, the tone of his voice, the way he engages with him.

Certain human emotions—particularly empathy and other advanced emotions—must be learned through experience. Some things, such as fear and some basic rage, are present early in life. You don't have to have special nurturing to feel scared or become enraged. But empathy and love and compassion—these require experience to express themselves. Such refined emotions are not wired into our nervous systems. The experience of being loved and protected is the beginning of empathy. And what happens next is very, very important.

Communicating Empathy

By eight or nine months, a baby is learning to read and respond to various emotional signals. Johnny notices his mother's facial expression when she gets excited, when she's happy, when she's annoyed—and he experiences and responds differently to those varying expressions. When Mommy looks annoyed, he pulls away a little bit. But when she gives a big smile, he gives a big smile back. When Mommy expresses surprise with a breathy "Oh," he also makes a sound of surprise. When she gasps in fear, Johnny may look around cautiously as if to say, "What's happening here?"

What's going on? Mother and baby are exchanging emotional signals. From this the baby makes two important discoveries: first, that another person is separate from him and part of the outside world; and second, that the other person is part of an out-side *emotional* world.

Making these discoveries is essential for the development of empathy. If he is to experience his mother's feelings as distinct from his own, a child has to know there's another person out there who is not part of himself; if he doesn't have this knowledge, he tends to project himself onto others and feel that we're all part of him. To avoid over-identifying and to be able to recognize that someone is different, a child needs to experience the feelings of others as coming from outside himself, not from within himself. He needs to recognize that they are Mommy's feelings or Daddy's feelings, not his. In addition, he has to learn to read emotional signals if he is to develop the ability to empathize. He has to sense, not just intellectually understand, the difference between anger and joy—actually sense it and feel it in his body.

When we empathize with a person, the process is intuitive and quick. Our bodies respond and our voice tones respond *before* we actually figure out what the other person is feeling. Only then do we recognize intellectually that the other person is feeling angry or sad or happy or joyful. We learn these quick, emotional responses to another person's feelings through repeated exchanges with others, and this process is a foundation for empathy.

Playing, Laughing, and Working Together

If that early phase of learning to recognize others as separate from ourselves goes well, Johnny and Suzie move on to another stage. The children begin to form a complex sense of themselves and to engage in shared social problem solving. From about ten to eighteen months, this begins in partnership with their parents.

One day, toddler Johnny takes Daddy by the hand and leads him to the toy area and points to the truck he wants. Daddy, nodding empathetically and warmly, reaches the truck down from its shelf and hands it to his son. Success!

Success at enlisting parents in a shared goal is the beginning of learning to cooperate, to work together. We see children doing it with their peers, too. By eighteen months, children are playing together, building sand castles together, taking turns going up the slide, and giggling together at shared jokes. They aren't just knocking each other down, as you might see in a fourteeen-month-old, or starting to cry themselves when another child gets upset. Now they are actually sharing games and humor together.

I did a study of toddlers with William Press, a colleague at the National Institutes of Health, and we found that we could identify a stage at about eighteen months when children began sharing humor. (Some kids even get there a little earlier than that.) At this stage, they can actually participate in extended cooperation as well as identify and react to feelings. They copy and begin to identify with others. They can work together to solve problems.

What does shared problem solving have to do empathy? You probably noticed that I've called it shared *social* problem solving. The process has to do with getting along together in social settings, whether that's at home, on a play date, or in the playground. It takes empathy to work with another person who has his own emotional challenges and joys. We see it happening when we observe repeated efforts at communicating about a project. In other books, I have called these efforts "circles of communication." In an eight-month-old, you see only three or four circles in a row, that is, a gesture, a response, another gesture, and so on for a few times. But by eighteen months, kids may move through as many as fifty or sixty such circles as they try to play together with a toy or ride on a pretend train.

Researchers have reported seeing the first signs of altruism—concern for someone else that is not primarily motivated by self-interest—appear at around eighteen months. A child will go up to his mother, for example, and pat her on the arm if she looks upset. If another child bumps himself and begins to whimper, the child may give him a hug or pat him on the back. This behavioral altruism is distinct from empathy because empathy requires an intellectual as well as emotional understanding of how another person is feeling. It requires a real concern about the other person. This early altruistic response is more basic than that, but is a precursor to empathy.

We don't really know whether the altruism shown by a toddler who pats his mother or hugs a crying child is a copy-cat behavior because he saw his parents do it or whether it is a sincerely felt, empathetic response. But when Johnny and Suzie reach out to comfort another child, they must reach outside themselves. Whether they are doing it because they're copying it or because they truly feel it, they see that their actions can help another person feel better. It may not be true empathy yet, but it is certainly a dramatic landmark on that path.

Empathy in Words

The next big step toward empathy occurs when we see children engaging in imaginative play. This happens between eighteen months and about two or three years of age, as their words come in. Children begin to involve their parents or siblings in shared pretending. Sophie might pretend that her mother is a hungry bear and she's feeding her. Or she and another child might pretend to be mother and baby bear.

How does empathy develop from shared pretend play? In games of make-believe, children are operating at a symbolic level, at the level of words and ideas. They are beginning to share their world with someone else. Sophie and her mother or Sophie and her friend are part of the same world of shared images, a world of hungry bears. They are sharing feelings of hunger and nurturing or satisfaction, all through the bear play. This takes the engagement seen in a four-month-old baby who shares smiles with mother to a new level. Now, bears or dolls or dinosaurs are smiling together or are sad together. By sharing feelings symbolically, a child is not only beginning to feel empathetically but also beginning to think empathetically. In imaginary play, kids experiment with feelings, assigning changing roles to toys to try out what those feelings are like. One doll can be a mean teacher or a mean parent, and moments later a nice teacher, a funny boy, a sad girl, and so on.

Imaginative play lets a child use his creativity to explore the world of feelings safely. By pretending a stuffed bear is a mean teacher, he begins to understand what it feels like when someone is mean to you. By changing the same toy into a funny character, he discovers how laughter can defuse hurt feelings. He can imagine what his toy character (and by extension another child) feels like when he's hurting, or when he's happy, and sees those feelings as separate from his own. By playing on the floor with his battered toys, he is learning to be empathetic.

Logic and Empathy

Soon after pretend play, a child learns to build logical bridges between ideas and to think in a cause-and-effect way: "I'm happy because you gave me a toy." "I'm sad because you won't let me go out and play." When his mother asks, "Why are you so mad today?" he can say, "Because I want that new toy you won't buy me."

Empathy goes to another level when a child can reason not only about how he's feeling but also how another person is feeling.

Not only can he say, "I'm mad because . . . ," he can say, "Mommy, why are you mad?"

At this point, a child is beginning to separate his world from the world of his parents. He can distinguish his internal world from his mother's world and still be concerned about hers. He can take an interest in her, be concerned, and want to know why she is happy or sad, yet at the same time understand that he doesn't share those feelings. He can then begin relating your feelings to his and measuring his experience against yours.

Now a child not only can investigate feelings and figure out the why of his own emotions—"I feel sad when Mommy leaves for work," but he also begins to see the why of other people's feelings: "Mommy feels happy when I snuggle in her lap," "Daddy laughs when I make funny faces." At first, these connections are basic and simple, seen in black and white: A lost toy equals sadness; early bedtime equals anger.

At the next stage of development, these stark equations will begin to change into subtler shades of gray. Now a child will move into a more complicated stage of empathy where he will explore multiple reasons for his feelings and those of others.

Jennifer was moving into this stage when her parents moved to a new town. They prepared their daughter for the move with lots of conversations about how nice their new neighborhood was going to be, and that its nearby playground "even has a pool." They talked about Jennifer's new room, and about the new friends she was going to have. "I can't wait to move," Jennifer's mom said often. "It's going to be so much fun."

So Jennifer was surprised to find her mommy crying in the empty kitchen after the moving truck had left and the family was about to climb in the car and follow them.

"Mommy, you're *so* sad. You're crying!" Jennifer said.

"I'm sad to be leaving our old house," her mom replied.

"But you're happy about the new house, too. You're happy and sad," Jennifer reminded her, giving her mom a pat. In the middle of a complex situation, Jennifer was able to see that her mom could experience two apparently conflicting feelings about the move. Jennifer, too, would experience these feelings after they arrived at the new house, and they all missed their old routines and friends. "I'm a little bit sad about our old house," Jennifer told her mom one night. "But I am a lot glad about my new room." Jennifer has reached the stage where she can recognize degrees of ambiguity and conflict in feelings, a critical component of empathy.

Parents who have some insight into their own feelings, and can modulate them and express ambivalence, make it easier for their children to develop this more complex kind of empathy. If you say you are exhausted and feel cranky after a hard day at work, but that you feel good because you have finished an important project, your child can begin to expand his thinking about feelings and develop a more mature version of empathy. He can then explore the shades of gray between feelings, the different reasons for feelings, and ways that different people respond to feelings. He will begin to see the world in a more complex way, as he grows up, and be able to take different perspectives, an essential life skill.

It's Never Too Late

For most of us, learning empathy began early in life and the learning proceeded through predictable stages. Remember, though, that with empathy, as with the other great kid characteristics, the child has a chance at each stage of development to regroup; a chance to practice; a chance to learn from experience. And you as a parent have a chance to create experiences for your children that will help them master earlier stages that they may not have gotten down the first time around. As you read this, don't worry if you feel that if you didn't do the right thing in the first six months of your child's life, or didn't nurture empathy at age two, your child will never learn. The ability to care how another person feels—like the ability to love, to be just and fair—can be developed any time, though it's a little harder the older you get if the foundations haven't been built in your earlier relationships.

But kids can catch up. Take Christopher, a child who grew up in an orphanage in Eastern Europe and came to this country when he was four. He had not had any of the experiences that enable a high level of empathy. He had lived with emotional and physical deprivation at a critical time in his development. At first, he operated in survival mode, just trying to get food and some basic affection. He appeared manipulative and impersonal in his relationships, and he sought warmth from almost any adult—which was hard on his adoptive parents.

But we have found that by working intensely with children like Christopher, providing extra nurturing, loving, and warmth, figuring out their sensitivities and fears, and helping them feel secure, that they, too, can learn to be highly empathetic adults. It will take a Christopher many years in a very warm and nurturing family situation to become trusting and empathetic. It may well require therapy. But it is never too late.

Empathy on the Playground

Have you ever watched a group of children clustered around a jungle gym or a swing set? They stand, heads together, talking intently. Or they play games, taking turns, intensely discussing the rules, fighting about whose turn comes next. Their discussions and games are about important questions: Who's in? Who's out? Who's up? Who's down? Who's first? Who's last? These kids, from ages eight to ten or so, are deep in the world of playground politics.

When children become part of a social group at school. They spend a huge amount of time calibrating how they fit in with the other children. Who's smartest? Who's the second most smart? Who's the best soccer player? Who's best at numbers? Who's the best dancer? Who's the cutest? Who's the funniest?

We all know that our eight-, nine-, or ten-year-olds are calculating their own position in the social hierarchy of the playground, constantly comparing themselves to all the other children. Sometimes it's very painful if our children feel they are not as good as other children at certain things. I like to tell parents whose child might be taking a social hit at this point and is feeling disappointed or dejected because he isn't the best at everything that this is the healthiest thing that can happen. Experiencing these feelings now is far better for children than if they learn them for the first time at age nineteen and experience their first rejections by a boyfriend or girlfriend or by a good friend. Disappointments that come the first time to a late teenager are harder to deal with. At age nine, disappointment can be alleviated by crying in the safety of home; that doesn't happen or doesn't help at age nineteen.

An important thing for parents to understand is that without disappointment and sadness, a child can't learn to have true joy or a true sense of self. He can't have a true identity, because what defines our identity and defines our sense of self and our joy in life is the ability to test ourselves in many situations.

Angela wanted more than anything to sing the "Tomorrow" song from *Annie* in the year-end play her class put on for parents. But the teacher gave that coveted role to Angela's friend, Tina. Angela was devastated. Because she cried right in front of her classmates, she had to deal with her humiliation as well as her disappointment. Meanwhile, Tina was thrilled. This may seem like a minor drama to adults, but to Angela it was as monumental as not getting a coveted promotion would be to her dad. All her parents could do was to say, "We're so sorry, we know how it feels."

Angela's disappointment ebbed, and she participated in the play with enthusiasm. She even cheered when Tina sang the "Tomorrow" song beautifully. But she did not forget the pain of losing the part, and that very real experience will contribute to making her a great kid. Later on in life, Angela will be able to comfort others who have suffered disappointments from a place of real understanding. When she says, "I know just what that feels like," she will be speaking from experience. If everything always goes smoothly, such understanding does not have a chance to develop.

A sense of self is defined by the different feelings we experience. Without experiencing disappointment, we won't know what we most want or most miss. Without anger, we won't know what frustrates us. Without experiencing excitement, we won't know what thrills us. Each of these feelings, in turn, also defines a new realm of empathy. We come to recognize that other people have these experiences and feelings, too, quite separate from our own. If we've experienced grief, we can empathize with others when it happens to them. It deepens our humanity. If everything has been too easy for us, we can say the words, "I know how you feel," but they are empty and meaningless.

Group Empathy

Although playground politics can be harsh, being part of a social group allows children to broaden their feelings of empathy for other children. Schoolchildren are finely tuned to the nuances of their groups, whether it's a group on the playground, their third-grade class, or their mixed-gender neighborhood gang whose members get together to play on Saturday mornings. They can sense the mood of their classrooms, whether it is a mood of seriousness and hard work or of mischief and merriment. They can sense the spirit of a larger group of individuals, such as the solidarity of the Brownie troop when "Taps" is played at the end of the meeting, or the raucous joy of the soccer team as players jump up and down when someone scores a goal. They are able to take the temperature of the group and to participate in its shared feelings.

This sense of belonging also promotes empathy. Kids begin to look beyond their immediate family and identify with their friends at school. They can say to themselves, "I belong to such and such a team" or "My school is Upper Valley Elementary." The child identifies with the group and cares about the group.

This empathy with a larger social group is a critical part of the glue that holds societies together. Empathy begins with individuals, but extends to the larger group that shares certain feelings, goals, and aspirations with us—our immediate family, our soccer team, our church or temple or mosque, our state, our country.

Groups also create problems. Groups are the basis for one gang's war with another gang, or one nation's war with another. We all need to extend empathy to other human groups who populate the earth to feel a global identification beyond our family or national identification. When we see children become so overly concerned with their little peer group that they exclude others, creating an "us vs. them" mentality, we can help them expand their empathetic range beyond their group of "cool kids" by asking them how some of the "not-so-cool kids" might be feeling.

It's healthy and helpful to extend the child's empathetic range to individuals who are not like him in race, religion, or physical or mental abilities. In this way, each parent can have a small effect on global conflict by raising an empathetic child. If your child has a Sudanese friend at school, he will experience real feelings of empathy when he hears a news story about famine in Sudan. If your child has a disabled friend, he will be more aware of the struggles facing the disabled.

Children need to experience people unlike themselves in a nonthreatening setting, because when they feel threatened they resort to all-or-nothing, black-and-white thinking. (Of course, adults do this too, as we did after September 11 when the sight of someone wearing a turban or a keffiyeh could trigger immediate feelings of panic before a more reasoned response set in.) A diverse set of friends or classmates provides opportunities for understanding—and feeling empathy for—other cultures.

Empathy Through Self-Reflection

When Ethan was six, his mom and dad divorced, and when he was nine, his mom remarried. Ethan took his time warming up to his stepfather, but once he did, he enjoyed the relationship and came to depend on the funny and reliable adult man who had moved into his house and into all their lives.

Then, when Ethan was in fifth grade, tragedy struck his family. His stepfather, Tom, died prematurely of a heart attack. As kids will, Ethan turned to his friends for solace, acting with them as if nothing much had happened, although he became a quieter and more reflective child after his loss.

Two years later, Ethan's friend Lucas also suffered a loss. Lucas's dad died after a long battle with cancer. Because Ethan had experienced a great loss and had learned to step into someone else's shoes, he was a comforting presence for his friend. Ethan noticed that Lucas was getting mad a lot, turning away from his buddies, picking fights, and falling behind in his schoolwork. Ethan recognized that he had been in a similar place when his stepdad died.

His mom overheard him talking to his friend on the phone one afternoon not long after Lucas's father's death: "Look, Luke, I know it's tough, what you're going through. Okay, it's not the same as it was for me when David died. I mean, you knew your dad all your life. I only knew David for a couple of years. But I know it's hard. You've got to say how you feel, man, you've just got to admit that you're sad."

Later, Lucas's mom told Ethan's mom that this understanding from his friend had broken through and helped Lucas begin to mourn the loss of his beloved father.

You may be thinking, "Wait a minute, these are seventh grade boys. There's no way they talked to each other or supported each other that way." But this is a true story. As early as their preteen years, children reach another, more complex level: the ability to empathize in a truly reflective manner. This means the ability to have an organized sense of self; to know who they are; to have gone through self-defining experiences around sadness and happiness and disappointment. This helps a child or adult be a truly great friend; and, through coming to terms with personal experiences, he can understand not just individuals but entire groups of people. It's a hard thing to achieve because it involves reflecting on yourself and your own feelings and on other people at the same time. You're not losing who you are as you identify with others; you don't remove yourself from them to protect yourself.

To empathize truly with another person's sadness or despair, we must have experienced at least some of this ourselves, though not so intensely that it derails us or disorganizes us or throws us into depression. There is a difference between sadness and disappointment, which we can work through, and true depression, which tends to engulf a person, though some people come out of that with an even deeper sense of empathy. Understanding these things begins on the childhood pathways we have just walked along.

Among the things that contribute to a great kid, empathy is a megaquality. Therefore, it is not surprising that lack of empathy characterizes a range of problems. At its extreme, a lack of empathy involves antisocial personality problems; these are exemplified by the sociopath who sees people or animals as things, such as a car or a table, rather than as sentient beings with feelings of their own. In its milder forms, it shows as a certain callousness, a self-centered view of life. A child who laughs when another falls down or taunts a losing team might need a kindly reminder of the feelings of others.

False Empathy

The ability to put oneself in the other person's shoes can be simulated. We've experienced adults who are shrewd at reading people. They are extraordinary at working the crowd at a cocktail party or at persuading people to buy this or that product. During their dating years, they might have been great at seducing this or that person. During their working years, they became skilled at getting people to do what they want them to do. But such people may have trouble with intimate long-term relationships because their ability to read and understand people is used, for the most part, in a self-serving way. They exploit people and take advantage of them. They have great "people skills," but they use them for their own selfish purposes, not truly to understand others. This is not empathy; this is manipulation. Children, too, often learn how to manipulate to get their own way; for purposes of their own, they discover how to fake interest or concern about another child or a parent.

In recent years, there has been a lot of talk about the narcissism, the self-centeredness, of our culture. I have to wonder whether the characteristic we are talking about in this chapter is somehow less supported these days by our families. Are we spending enough time with our children, or are our kids being cared for by others, people who are not continuous in their lives and can't establish the same degree of empathy and caring? We can teach language or motor skills, and even self-control, but to be empathetic you have to feel empathy—which means you have to have experienced empathy and intimacy yourself. You can't offer it to others in a genuine way if you don't know it yourself.

Lifelong Empathy

In adolescence, when kids are often thought to be especially self-centered, empathy continues to develop. Closer friendships replace many family relationships in high school and beyond. An intimate relationship allows for new levels of empathy. If we are lucky, we have the experience of falling in love with the whole world as we fall in love with one person. We have often heard someone say that loving someone "has made me a better person." And so it has.

As adolescents find powerful affinities with others outside their families and form new bonds with them, they begin operating on a larger stage. They see more of the injustices of the world, and they may rail at their parents for being complacent and insensitive in the face of how awful and unfair things are. Yet as they enter college and take on jobs and new obligations, these same adolescents will gain a new empathy for their parents, a greater understanding of their perspectives. A friend of mine tells me that she recently found a book she had given her mother years ago for Christmas, when she was a freshman in college. The dedication read, "Now that that I have spent a semester away from you, I begin to see the lessons in peace and kindness that you have been trying to teach me all along."

Having a family of your own offers a chance to pass along the lessons of empathy—or sometimes a second chance to learn those lessons for the first time through the love you have for your children. Raising children deepens empathy in ways you never could have anticipated. We recognize our children as part of ourselves, but we also see them as separate—the precondition for feeling empathy. Resonating with our kids' joys and sorrows, we broaden and deepen our own empathic range.

Empathy, whether for children, for one's spouse, or for one's friends, deepens over time. In adulthood, empathy can be both painful and joyous. Laura, a thirty-year-old living and working on her own far from her family, faced the news that her mother's annual mammogram revealed a small cancer. After the initial terror and disbelief had passed, Laura found herself comforting her mother as her mother had once comforted her. She put aside her own fear and listened to her mother's fear. She held her father's hand when he poured out his feelings of helplessness as they waited for the biopsy report. When the lab results came in showing that the cancer had not spread to the lymph nodes, Laura could share in her parents' vast sense of relief and joy.

As we grow older, new experiences deepen our empathy with others. For example, having an illness helps us understand the feelings of others who are ill. As we experience losses, we see the cycle of life in a new way. We may become more involved—as many people do in adulthood and middle age—in political, social, and environmental issues and so extend our empathy beyond national and generational boundaries.

RAISING AN EMPATHETIC CHILD

Empathy is the hallmark of a great kid, but it's one of the hardest traits for a child to acquire. Although all children are born with an innate need to relate to others, they need examples and encouragement to be able to feel themselves in other person's shoes. This is a complicated cognitive and emotional task that grows and develops over time, with your help. Reminding your child simply to behave in a way that's "nice" toward others isn't enough.

Each time you tune into your child's feelings and let him know that you understand that he's in the grip of powerful emotions, you validate his sense that he is not alone, that he is not unworthy. By communicating that even scary feelings of rage or shame are legitimate, and shared by every human being, over time you will teach your child to tolerate these emotions in himself and eventually empathize with them in others.

Even before a child has words at his disposal, you can teach him lessons in empathy by simply mirroring his facial expressions. Most of us instinctively grimace in sympathy when we see a colicky four-month-old's eyes squeeze tight in pain; or we beam at a wiggly, happy baby when he bicycles his little legs in joy at our approach. Your heightened facial expressions and vocal tones, which reflect or mimic your baby's emotions, provide your preverbal child with an externalized "picture" of his feelings. In this way, your baby begins to feel the deep satisfaction of having his feelings understood.

Although your one-year-old won't understand many of the words that you use as you mirror his feelings, the tone of your voice will communicate your empathy. When you cluck your tongue and sympathetically murmur, "Oh, I can tell that your tummy's hurting s-o-o-o much," or shake your head from side to side and tenderly say, as you smooth his hair away from his forehead, "Honey, you don't look like a happy camper today," your baby experiences your caring in what he sees, hears, and feels in your touch. As you express your own feelings in reaction to his, your baby will respond to your overtures, perhaps by reaching up for a cuddle or by whimpering a little. These exchanges give the child the experience of your feelings.

With an eighteen-month-old, a little dramatizing of your feelings will help get them across. If your son pushes a toy out of your hands while the two of you are dipping into the toy box, you might, for example, put your hands on your hips and softly growl "Hmmmm . . . ," just as the cartoon character Marge Simpson does when she views the antics of her son Bart.

Between the second and third years of life, as you follow your child's lead in his little make-believe games, you can encourage him to experience and express a gradually wider range of feelings. If his dramas routinely feature "good soldiers" and "happy bears," you might introduce a little agitation into the plot. Hide a soldier, or block the parade. Let your child or his soldiers protest and push your toys away. Shielding a child from negative emotions during play does him no favors. Similarly, if his soldiers are getting stuck in angry or assertive behavior and keep bopping each other on the head, after a while let a toy puppy scamper into the drama (you might even give him the same moniker as your beloved family pet) and give a wounded soldier some tender licks. As you allow a wider range of emotional themes, and then play out both sides of a feeling in pretend play, you'll be helping him become more aware of all his feelings in a safe, supportive way.

It's important to realize, however, that both you and your child may feel anxious when negative feelings come into play. Some children—and their parents, too—are reluctant to assume the "bad guy" role in their play, and they need to approach conflict slowly. Other children want to assume bad guy or monster or tyrant personnas in their dramas because they're trying to understand the emotions of jealousy or anger or competition that overwhelm them at times. They may be very afraid of their own aggressive feelings and, in their play, take on roles in which they wield power so that someone else won't act aggressively toward them—a best-defense-is-a-good-offense tactic. Since those situations permit your child to explore scary feelings in safety, it's important not to shut down these themes as they emerge in conversation and play. They will need limits set only if their negativity is translated into destructive behavior. By extending your empathy to your child across a broad range of emotions, by not shutting down emotional themes that challenge you, you help him accept these emotions in himself.

You can help preschool and young schoolchildren become aware of their emotions in reality-based ways, too. "Thinking about Tomorrow" games enable children to imagine real situations and how they might feel. Questions such as "How will you feel tomorrow if your soccer team doesn't win?" or "Will your teacher be angry with you if you keep on forgetting your lunch money?" help your child anticipate feelings that he might avoid facing on his own.

Although some children can begin to appreciate the feelings of others at this age, the ability to empathize with how another person is likely to feel doesn't really develop until around the ages of eight to fourteen. Without passing judgment on your child's feelings, it's important to let him tell you how he thinks his playmates or siblings might feel in certain situations. Encourage your child to express his understanding of another's emotions, even if it reveals a not-so-flattering aspect of his personality.

Let's say, for example, that you and your eight-year-old are shooting the breeze after the dinner dishes have been cleared away. Perhaps your child will share some of the politicking that's emerging around the playground, telling you with glee how she and her friends made fun of the way a new girl at school jump-ropes.

"How do you think Meghan feels when you snicker at her?" you might ask. (Note that you don't rush to judgment and stifle the conversation by saying "You girls really shouldn't make Meghan feel badly.") Your daughter might reply,

"Oh, I don't think she minds."

"Why not?"

"Because even if we laugh at her, we're still letting her jump with us."

And you know what? Your daughter may be correct. But you might then pose a question that would enable her to appreciate Meghan's feelings in that situation: "Honey, do you think Meghan likes being part of your group or she likes having all of you laugh at her?"

If your daughter replies, "Well, I guess she doesn't like us laughing at her, but she wants to be part of our group so she puts up with it," you've helped her take a giant step into empathy. The time will eventually come when she'll avoid mocking another child, even when she knows it can temporarily feel intoxicating or powerful. This doesn't occur, even under the best of circumstances, until about ages eight to ten and beyond, when children actually learn to operate in two worlds. At that point, they will be able to use their own feelings, and how they like to feel, as a standard for their behavior toward others.

A particularly empathic eight-year-old who is moved by the television programs he sees about people surviving a tsunami might be encouraged to imagine himself and his friends escaping from the waves or finding food for their fellow villagers. This might lead him actually to look for ways to help. Such conversations with an adolescent often focus on people living in famine-plagued countries or in societies where people are imprisoned unfairly or women can't go to school. Books such as *To Kill a Mockingbird, The Diary of Anne Frank,* and *Oliver Twist* can stimulate discussions about injustice and prejudice against all those who are "different," opening up new avenues for empathy.

Encouraging Empathy

1. Empathize with your child. Empathy comes from being empathized with.
2. Help him become aware of his own feelings and to express them. Allow him to express a full range of feelings.
3. Help him tune in to others' feelings by making your feelings clear. Let them show in facial expressions and voice.
4. Having him take an interest in other people's feelings by using his own as a standard for comparison.
5. Let your child experience—in safety—all kinds of situations. Encourage him to use his imagination to stretch beyond the experiences he's already had.

Empathy never ends. It is a continually expanding dimension of life, and its foundations are set in these stages I've described. As your children grow, you can help them grow empathy by engaging in each stage with them. Laugh with your baby. Get down on the floor and play make-believe with your toddler. When your child gets excited or anxious, ask him how he feels and why he feels that way. In elementary school, make sure he meets a variety of other children and that he makes good friends. When your child reaches the stage of thinking reflectively, ask his opinions. Support his friendships and listen to his passions. All these daily experiences, and many more, promote the quality of empathy that will help make your child a great kid.

3

Curiosity
An Inquiring Mind

. . . .

When four-year-old Carter's aunt took him to the Smithsonian Natural History Museum, she was hoping to show him the big cats in a new exhibit there. But Carter had other ideas. He was interested in one thing and one thing only: seeing the dinosaurs.

"But you saw the dinosaurs last time we were here," his aunt said.

Carter didn't have time to stand and debate this question. As they got off the escalator, Carter pulled his aunt's hand. "Come *on,*" he said, as he dragged her past the towering elephant in the rotunda and into the dinosaur hall.

Carter's aunt gave up—for the moment, anyway—her plan to show him the big cats. He was on a mission, and she decided to join him on it. As they looked at skeletons and dioramas of vanished creatures, Carter was utterly engaged and excited by what he saw. As his aunt read him the labels on the exhibits, he repeated the odd-sounding words: *stegosaurus, brontosaurus, brachiosaurus, T. rex.*

The aunt's instinct had told her to follow Carter's interest in and passion about a particular thing. Carter may well grow out of his curiosity about dinosaurs, or he may continue this interest throughout his life and even make a career out of paleontology. But right now, the most important thing that the adults in Carter's life can do is to engage his enthusiasm, help him expand his interests, and nurture the powerful energy for learning that curiosity creates.

When the pair reached the end of the dinosaur display, Carter's aunt said, "Okay, now that we've seen these guys, let's go look at the big cats."

Carter agreed this time. They walked fairly quickly through the new exhibit, glancing at the tigers and leopards. But Carter's curiosity was awakened when he saw a snow leopard. "That looks like a great big Jonesie," Carter said, referring to his pet cat. "Read it to me," he said to his aunt, pointing to the label on the display. His aunt began to read about the shy Himalayan leopards—and Carter's attention was caught. Once again, he was off and learning.

THE POWER OF CURIOSITY

Curiosity—an interest in the world and how and why things work in it—is a fundamental trait for a great kid. Curiosity makes an infant turn her head toward her mother's voice; curiosity leads toddlers to bang on a xylophone and build block towers; curiosity sends a schoolchild to climb fences or into a neighbor's yard to meet the child who has just moved there; curiosity leads the adolescent to reprogram her computer; curiosity leads the college student to stay late at the chemistry lab, sends a cub reporter deeper into a news story that will shape her career, or someday will send a retiree to dig up bones in the western desert (those dinosaurs again).

Curiosity, in fact, is such a reliable force in a small child that a parent's job is mainly to keep her safe, without dampening that inquisitive spirit. Asking why, how, who, and what happens next are central pursuits at every stage of life. Curiosity is the engine that starts that process; other important traits that we'll discuss in this book—including logic, creativity, and discipline—keep the process going.

Letting a Child Take the Lead

Carter's aunt had the good sense to follow her nephew's energetic insistence on seeing the dinosaurs at the museum. She also knew that to follow his lead didn't have to mean simply doing whatever he did. She took her cue from him, but she also built on it. When she led him into a new area of possible interest, his knowledge of the world broadened.

Encouraging curiosity means tuning in to and building on your child's interest, beginning when she is very young. Let's say your toddler is taking apart her new stuffed duck to see what makes the quacking sound. Do you whisk the toy away or do you let her follow her search? Or perhaps you show her just where to pinch to make the sound again.

In almost any activity you can see your child's curiosity leading her into new challenges. The important thing is to encourage this and not try to direct her play. You may not love following your toddler to see what mischief she is into next, or cleaning up globs of finger paint or a collapsed block tower, but you'll welcome your child's joy. By taking pleasure in your child's natural interests, you can find opportunities for her to pursue them further, perhaps with a friend who shares her interests. As they grow up, curious children will come up with new ideas, new questions about how things work, how other people feel, and why people behave as they do. They will begin to understand the world not only from their own points of view, but also from other people's perspectives. By suggesting places to look and ways to explore a passionate interest, parents and other adults can be great allies for expanding a child's interest in understanding the world.

The mathematician and educational theorist Seymour Papert, in his book *Mindstorms,* told of the way his curiosity developed as a child. As his interest in mechanical devices grew, he literally "fell in love with gears." He makes very clear that a child's curiosity has deep emotional resonance. Such delight in inquiry cannot be taught, it can only be encouraged (and admired and enjoyed!).

Curiosity and Intellectual Breadth

For a child—as for an adult—channeling curiosity into scientific or creative inquiry means having a robust set of skills for reasoning, reflecting about, and understanding the world. This includes the mastery of intellectual tasks, such as solving puzzles and math and technical problems, designing software, or a legal case. But true inquiry also involves imagination and emotional insight, being able to understand another person's point of view, to recognize ambiguous situations, and to listen clearly to one's own deepest emotions. Intellectual breadth includes not just scientific and abstract thinking, but also, in emotional and spiritual terms, curiosity, a search for meaning.

The very first puzzle for a baby is to decipher her mother's smiles or scowls. As the baby grows, the breadth of the world she must understand expands; she engages every one of her senses to fathom the people she loves and trusts. She wonders where they are and is puzzled if her smile does not bring a smile in return.

A toddler's new dexterity and mobility expand the reach of her experience. She wonders what's inside a box that's out of her reach on the top shelf. She gestures to Mommy to take the box off the shelf, sit down on the carpet with her, and help her find out. By following the toddler's signals, the parents can help her understand cause and effect. They can encourage her to move her explorations along into new territory and allow her a wide range, short of actual danger. (Electrical outlets are just as fascinating as wind-up toys.) All this happens *before* she has started to express her curiosity in words—although those relentless "why" questions are just around the corner.

Exploring Through Connecting

Curiosity is the quality that urges a child to keep on finding out more, to connect actions with outcomes, people with feelings. *Wondering why* is the powerful engine that drives discovery— think of the biologist Rachel Carson, who wondered why the marshes and meadows had fallen silent, a question that would lead eventually to the book *Silent Spring* and the banning of DDT. Think of cosmologists looking for new galaxies, biologists and computer scientists mapping the human genome, psychiatrists and brain scientists exploring the landscape of the human mind.

The fuel that drives world-changing discoveries begins in childhood. Great kids are curious—and their curiosity enlarges their world and lights up their creativity. At the beginning, that process is encouraged in shared experiences with parents and other significant adults. No matter whether a child wants to go out and jump in a pile of autumn leaves in the backyard or is wondering why her mother looks sad today, she still needs co-operation from adults who help her express her questions. The key is for parents to keep challenging their children to figure things out. If she wonders how an eggbeater works, let her try beating an egg. When a child says, "I want to go outside," don't just open the door. Ask why, and she will say, "Because I want to play in the leaves." Then her feeling, her wish, is connected to an idea. If she asks why you seem annoyed, don't just shrug; let her know about your feelings in ways she can understand.

Evoking Complex Answers

Parents can help encourage lively curiosity by asking questions. When Sam is playing with his trains, ask him questions: "What happens when you add the curved track? How long does it take to get all the way around? What made the caboose fall off?" Keep the inquiry going, and you encourage Sam's breadth of thinking.

Curiosity also underlies triangular thinking, which extends into multicausal thinking. To encourage triangular thinking, ask a child for different kinds of solutions to a problem. Don't supply an answer—challenge her to come up with it herself. Use the time-honored Socratic method: If the Lego tower won't stay up ask, "Well, what else can we do? How else can we build it?"

This kind of thinking operates in social settings, too. Tamara wants to play with Alice at her preschool, but Alice is always busy. Tamara wonders, "What else can I do?" She has noticed that Alice is good friends with Monica. "I wonder what would happen if I make friends with Monica, too?" she thinks. So clever Tamara invites Monica to play with her. Soon they are laughing and making a tent out of blankets and chairs. Alice feels a little jealous and wants to join in. Soon, all three girls are playing together.

We adults become involved in these kinds of triangular think-ing patterns all the time. We might call it "cunning" or even "manipulation," but it nevertheless shows breadth of thought. Cleverness and cunning in thinking—learning to solve problems in many ways—is a valuable skill for children. It helps them be-come more abstract and more reflective. Asking questions such as "What else can I do? What else might work?" is a habit that children will rely on throughout their lives.

As children get older and their verbal skills become more acute, adults can continue to encourage their passion for find-ing things out, for testing their ideas. You can encourage this through friendly debate, as early as age six or seven. When a child pressures you for something she wants, ask, "Can you prove to me why you're better than your brother at taking care of the dog?" "Show me what's the matter with your bike and why you think you need another."

When you ask kids to explain something in which they are powerfully invested, you are likely to get coherent, logical, care-fully thought out responses. (We know that all our kids are great lawyers when they're arguing for an extra five minutes before the bedroom light is turned off!) The point is that children will learn to apply those elaborate thought processes and that eloquence to other situations later on, whether they're writing a book report or analyzing a Civil War battle or solving a geometry problem.

The "wondering why" impulse really begins to get an intellec-tual workout in gray-area thinking. When a child tells you that a teacher is nice but sometimes unfair, or a hike was "very exciting but sometimes a little scary," she is showing gray-area thinking. Parents encourage this when they ask questions as their child's world broadens and becomes more complex. Questions can evolve from "Did Susie really deserve to be suspended?" to "Which character in that novel you read is your favorite?" and

"What happens if you disconnect both wires at once?" The questions can range from intellectual puzzles to a child's feelings and inquiry about her own place in the world.

Curiosity and Reflective Thinking

Powered by their curiosity and their deep emotional connections with things that interest them, children become curious not only about the world around them but also about the universe they hold inside—their feelings, dreams, disappointments, joys, and hopes. Children usually reach this stage of reflective thinking between the ages of ten and fourteen, depending on the way they have experienced the world so far and the way their nervous systems are developing.

True reflective thinking is fueled in the same way as early curiosity. Once again, as it did when your baby reached for a patterned mobile hung above her crib, this inner drive to find out about the world provides the energy, the incentive, for self-reflection. "Who am I?" All adolescents ask this question, and if we're honest, we also know that adults continue to ask it.

Reflective thinking in the emotional area means that a child can say things like, "Gosh, why am I so mad? I don't know why I feel this way—it's not usually the way I feel. Why is Jonathan's teasing bothering me so much? He's being just as idiotic as he was yesterday, when I could just laugh it off."

Such an inner dialogue is comparing a feeling of the moment—anger and hurt—to a baseline sense of self, an understanding of how one ordinarily feels and behaves. To do this, a child must think in two frames of reference at the same time.

Self-reflection will later enable an adolescent to say, "My friends are making fun of me and making me feel like a jerk for not drinking the beer (or not smoking), but I feel I'm doing the right thing."

This adolescent's insight is supported by a growing internal standard that allows her to compare her feelings of the moment to that standard. This ability balances her cravings and curiosity with moral behavior and judgment. It will be critically important in the teen years, when curiosity not guided by reflection can drive even a strong and balanced child toward some dangerous choices about alcohol, smoking, drugs, and sex. The self-exploration that characterizes reflective thinking comes along just at the right time!

A reflective child with an internal standard is able to explore her own thoughts, behavior, and judgment. It's as if she has an inner judge evaluating her decisions and her feelings. She's judging herself and others, not in a rigid, black-and-white, right-or-wrong way, but in terms of an evolving internal standard that changes as she gets older and more experienced. And what is this judging but asking, once again, those "why" questions powered by curiosity?

That inner judge comes in handy for writing essays, too. When asked to compare Mark Twain and Tolstoy, a student can answer not only the question "Which one reflected his age better, was a better spokesperson for the time he lived in?" but also, "Which one resonates with my experiences today?" A smart teacher might ask not just which writer reflected his age better, but which one's depiction of his age fits the way you see people behave in today's world.

Answering a question like that is a complicated, subtle academic task that involves evaluating your own worldview as well as comparing it to worldviews that you decipher in novels. Writing that essay will also require asking, "How can I explain this?" and then, "Did I get my point across effectively?" The ability to compose and evaluate your own essay means having criteria as to what an essay should be and inquiring whether you met that standard.

The enemy of this kind of complex thought, indeed the enemy of curiosity, is teaching only in a rote, memory-based way. There's no curiosity involved in memorizing, whether it's the nine-times-table or the periodic table. Healthy curiosity encourages kids to ask the why questions that underlie all knowledge—including multiplication and organic chemistry. Teaching through *thinking* engages, and unleashes, curiosity. When a teenager is motivated to evaluate her feelings, the logic of her essay, how well she studied (or didn't), whether or not she deserved to be punished by her parents or school for a particular activity, her understanding of the world will keep expanding.

The psychologist Ellen Langer, in her book *Mindfulness,* talks about "creative uncertainty." By this, she means that when ideas are presented in a conditional way, not simply as facts, creativity is more likely to be encouraged. We are more likely to explore ideas when they are seen as "possible" and not absolute truth.

Curiosity and "Theory of Mind"

An important achievement in intellectual development is called "theory of mind," which means the ability to figure out how other people think and feel and take other people's perspectives—something that we talked about when we discussed a great kid's development of empathy. Once again, it comes from that essential question, "Why?": "Why does Margaret think I'm teasing her when I'm only kidding? Maybe she's sensitive about certain things." This thinking involves not just self-knowledge, but also speculation about how another person's experience and world-view might be different.

If I want to know how someone else feels in a situation, first I've got to say to myself, "How would I feel in that situation? If I were jilted I know I'd feel sad and depressed. I wonder if Mark is also feeling sad and depressed? He's not *acting* that way, but he's kind of hyper, going up to every new girl in school and try-ing to meet them. I wonder if he's trying to cheer himself up by just acting the opposite. Or maybe he actually didn't like that girl that much. . . . Maybe he was just doing it because of peer pressure because she's popular."

Theory of mind enables a child to consider different hypothe-ses about how someone else might think or feel by putting her in the other person's situation—not necessarily assuming that the other person thinks or feels the way she does, but considering al-ternatives. This starts with the ability to have a sense of your own mind and emotions. Then you can project yourself into other people's shoes and consider, again, whether that's consistent with what you observe about how the person is behaving.

Inquiry at this high level involves being able to hold different perspectives in mind at the same time: your own perspective, what you observe about someone else's, and still other possibili-ties. This kind of highly refined curiosity characterizes academic and other kinds of work that require complex problem solving. It leads to ever-greater intellectual breadth.

NURTURING CURIOSITY

Great kids want to know how the world works and are eager to set out and explore new turf. With a small baby, don't merely

wait for her to respond to your overtures; instead, let her initiate the action. For instance, when you and your nine-month-
old sit down together on your living room rug, let her reach for
a rattle or squeaky toy; don't just hand it to her. Leave the rattle
a good three feet beyond the reach of your baby's outstretched
arms. She'll find it hard to resist the rattle's alluring shape, color,
motion, and sound. She'll likely reach out with a big smile on
her face and grab her prize, giving it a good shake. That first
glimmer of curiosity, of wanting to figure things out by herself
while she explores the world, can be dampened if you always
put the rattle in your baby's hand. Your baby is naturally drawn
to propel herself through "uncharted territory" toward the object of her desire. Her curiosity spurs her on, and as she coordi-
nates the movements of her back, arm, and leg muscles, she
literally hardwires her brain in ways that facilitate future intellectual and emotional growth.

Activities with two- or three-year-old toddlers that expand
their sensory experience of the world increase their curiosity.
Toys that are visually different from each other and involve different smells, sounds, and movements whet her curiosity in a
multitextured world. The toys needn't be elaborate; any parent
knows that a brightly painted box, a crunched up bit of wrap-
ping paper, "popable" bubble wrap, and drum-like oatmeal con-
tainers will often intrigue and entertain children engaged in
imaginary play at least as much as "real" toys. Pushing a child to
play with "educational" toys or insisting on strict neatness by
avoiding messes with paint or mud are sure ways to dampen
that inner engine of curiosity.

Always keep in mind that you want to work off your child's
innate pleasures and not dictate what those pleasures should be.
It's fine to bring out toys or to suggest activities that you think
she might be interested in, but then back off and simply follow

her lead. Don't make the mistake of orchestrating play in an attempt to challenge your child.

By the time she's four or five years old, you may find that your youngster is fascinated by blocks and miniature toys of all sorts. She's apt to orchestrate lots of pretend play around these, running buses up and down roads and past houses and schools constructed of wooden blocks. As you follow her lead and zoom your car behind hers en route to the zoo, try to have a block or doll "accidentally" obstruct the path. See whether this will cause her to explore the alternate routes to the zoo that still remain open. You can have fun together when you build obstacle courses that will challenge her ingenuity and help her stretch her muscles in new ways. As she becomes more physically coordinated, her curiosity in the world will be increased because she is able to explore fresh turf.

There are few better ways of enticing a kindergartner's curiosity than going for a nature walk. The two of you might get on your knees and see what the woods look like from the point of view of a fawn, or she might put her nose to the ground to spy on an ant's perspective. As you explore the city together when she's a little older, you'll continue to enable her to make new discoveries. By the time your child is nine years old or so, you can let her lead during some of your urban explorations. Let her point out the best place to transfer trains. There will be more and more activities where she's got a good shot at trumping you.

A child's innate curiosity develops best when parents listen. *If you want to promote an inquiring mind and intellectual breadth, get your child's opinions.* "Well, what do you think? And why? Did you feel that way a few weeks ago, or last year?" or "How do you think you might think about it in the future?" Whether you're asking those questions of your thirteen-year-old, your eighteen-year-old, your twenty-year-old, or your thirty-year-old, you're increasing their intellectual breadth.

We constantly judge our children, telling them whether an essay is good or bad. How much better if instead we ask our children, "What do you think of that essay? How does that compare to the one you wrote a week ago? How would that compare to one you might write when you have more time?"

"Well, Mom, this one is pretty hurried, I guess. It's not quite what I could do if I had more time."

Now, that exchange is priceless! Your child is judging her own behavior! That's the kind of reflection that will set her up to go off to college or to a job. That's what we all need for an independent life. As adults, we must to be able to judge our own thoughts, our own behavior, and our own feelings.

One of the biggest impediments to curiosity is the anxiety or fear that some children have in trying out new experiences or exploring new options or ideas. One way to overcome your child's hesitancy is to tie it to something that is of immediate interest to her. If your child hates getting wet, let her make a boat to sail in a fountain or pool and then watch her forget about wet feet. If sixteen-year-old Oscar feels stymied by schoolwork and shows little curiosity about anything other than tinkering with the '88 Buick Le Sabre that he's just bought with his own hard-earned money, a parent might try building a conversational bridge to his passion. "Did recent hurricanes in the Gulf of Mexico or politics in Venezuela make the price of gas go up?" Oscar will likely ask, "What are you talking about? Did you read this in the newspaper?" These kinds of conversational gambits can successfully nab his interest in broader horizons because he may wonder whether outside forces will interfere with his plans for the car.

At any age, your child's interest in exploring new territories will build on her particular joys and pleasures. It's important to bear in mind, however, that when you try to rustle up curiosity you'll want to see that the challenges do not overwhelm her. If your teen is pressured to master the intricacies of French grammar in the weeks before she goes on a monthlong student exchange, she's likely to give up and say, "Oh, I'll just hang out with the American kids." On the other hand, if she's given a useful list of two- or three-word phrases that she can master and reliably use when she first meets French friends, your daughter is liable to use this new tool and actually become interested in speaking a new language because it delivers results and gives her pleasure.

Encouraging Curiosity

1. Let your baby explore her world within the limits of safety.
2. Follow your child's interests; encourage her with toys to take apart, paints to mix, water to splash about, woods to explore.
3. Arrange activities with varied sights, sounds, smells, textures, and a variety of social situations and playmates.
4. Help a fearful child overcome fears of the new or unknown; encourage her to explore new territory.
5. Ask your child for her opinions, ideas, solutions to problems.

Life is a process of continuing to explore new realms and mastering additional levels of thinking at all ages. That's why in many cultures the wise ones are the elders. It's not because they know more facts; it's because they infuse their thinking with more experience and keep moving into a deeper exploration of life's mysteries and meaning.

This continuous growth of intellect doesn't mean, of course, that every child is going to be an Einstein or every parent a Socrates. It does mean that we can *all* continue to make progress and move forward, slowly or in spurts, sparked by our curiosity and enriched by the breadth of our thinking. Great kids—curious kids—grow into adults with intellectual breadth.

4

Communication

The Transforming
Power of Language

·····················

A school bus stops at the corner near my house every afternoon at around three o'clock. Hoisting their overloaded backpacks, children from the elementary school spill through the doors. As they head toward their various houses, some shout to each other; others chat quietly. Some, who may have had a tough day, walk silently with their heads bowed. As they scatter into their neighborhood, I am struck by how much they are communicating to each other—and to any adults who happen to be watching. The shouts among a bunch of fifth-grade boys who have had a great scrimmage on the basketball court reinforce their connection with each other. The whispered secret shared by a couple of fourth-grade girls establishes their intimacy— and excludes another girl, who walks home feeling sad. The silent child may be shy, or scared, or sickly. But his posture and silence communicate eloquently that something's not quite right with him today.

As adults, we don't remember learning how to let others know our desires and fears, our disappointments and sorrows. But we all learned, as our kids must learn, to get our messages and our meaning across.

Communication involves not only mastering speech and being able to talk fluently—an incredible physical and intellectual accomplishment of its own—it also means mastering facial expression, gestures, and tone of voice. Just as important, it means being able to listen and to recognize the expressions and gestures of others. Without listening, we cannot respond appropriately, nor can we engage in dialogue. Communication means being able to exchange information not only verbally with speech and tone but also nonverbally through gestures.

When we say an adult is a "great communicator," we mean that he or she articulates thoughts, feelings, ideas, and visions. With a raised eyebrow, a smile, or a shrug, an effective communicator can convey information as eloquently as with words and tone. A great communicator also understands the reactions of other people and reads the subtleties and nuances of what they are saying as well as the feelings they express. He can speak to individuals or groups, have intimate conversations with loved ones, and negotiate effectively at work.

HOW LANGUAGE DEVELOPS

There have been many theories to explain this astonishing achievement. Some people theorize that the process is almost magical, that human beings have a genetic code that at a certain point in our development just kicks in and enables us to learn to speak and use language. Some of my colleagues have thought that grammar, a very important part of language, is basically innate and all we need are certain stimuli to press our language buttons or open our language modules so that all of a sudden we have language.

I believe that acquiring language is much more than the igniting of genetic potential by some sort of environmental stimulation. As my colleague Stuart Shanker and I explain in our book *The First Idea,* language is a developmental process that involves the working together of nature and nurture. As with the other traits we are discussing in this book, the ability to communicate develops through a series of stages.

Sounds with Meaning

In the first months of life, babies just look and listen. They take in the world and learn to be calm and regulated within it. As we talk to our little babies, we encourage them to look at our mouths. They see how our tongues move, and what do you know, they copy our tongue movements! If you stick out your tongue at a newborn baby, most babies will stick their tongues back out at you. We see this simple, early form of imitation long before we see complex social imitation. Babies are learning the first steps in communication when they look at our interesting mouths as we move them and make interesting sounds.

Before long, babies may begin making sounds back at us. By four to five months, or even at three months, they and their parents have developed a repertoire of vocal rhythms. We say "Mmmmmmm" and babble at them—and they babble back. In a kind of personal music, we almost make the sounds simultaneously.

John Holt, the writer and educational reformer, spent much time watching small children and wondering at their skills. "Why does a baby begin to make sounds in the first place?" he asks. "Is it instinctive, like crying? It seems not to be. A puppy raised apart from other dogs will know how to bark when he gets old enough, but the few children we know of who grew up without human contact grew up almost entirely mute . . . apparently it is from hearing people speak around them that babies get the idea of 'speaking.'"

Our babies are doing a lot more than making sounds as they hum and babble with us. They are practicing the movements of their mouths that produce the sounds. They are looking at us and connecting the sounds they are making and how their bodies are moving with what they are seeing us do. All the while, our babies are learning to distinguish and make different sounds—skills that will come in handy when they begin to form words. They are getting a picture of us and we are getting a picture of them. But even now, as we stand over their cribs or hold them in our arms and hum and gurgle with them, we are communicating.

All parents know that even a newborn is a communicator. His communication uses gestures, facial expressions, body postures, different emotional expressions, and tone of voice to convey information. Parents quickly learn to distinguish their baby's pain cry from his sleepy cry, his hungry cry from the sound he makes when he's startled. His communication is nonverbal, but it is real and effective. When parents hear a particular cry, they respond in a particular way, whether it is by changing his wet diaper, cuddling him, or feeding him. Later, when their baby begins to smile and reach out to pat Mommy's or Daddy's face, the parent responds with hugs, nuzzles, and laughter. The baby initiates an exchange, and the parents respond. That's communication.

A young mother takes a visiting friend into the nursery to meet her baby, a three-month-old named Anna. Anna awakened from a nap a few minutes ago and is still a little fussy. But she's very glad to see Mommy. Anna makes a high, cooing noise, pumps her plump legs three times, and reaches her hands into the air.

"That means hello, Mommy, I'm glad to see you," Anna's mother says. "I'm glad to see you, Anna-Banana," she says to her daughter.

The friend is a little surprised. She doesn't know much about babies, and Anna's vocalizations just sound like noises to her.

"I know, you think I'm crazy," Anna's mom says. "But she really does make different sounds for different feelings. I know she does. I can tell when she's upset or when she's happy."

"That's amazing," her skeptical friend says. She leans down into Anna's crib and nuzzles the baby's neck.

"Whooo!" Anna says as she rears her head back. She's a little startled, but she's still smiling.

"That's her way to say she's surprised," Anna's mom says.

Anna's mother is not some kind of baby genius. Parents who pay attention to their babies' vocalizations will tell you that the sounds, gestures, and motions their little ones make can be interpreted and understood.

And they're right. As little Anna is demonstrating, even young babies use gestures and sounds, which are the precursors to words, with intention. They have feelings they want to convey. As Anna's mom recognizes, her daughter uses one sound for "I'm angry" and another for "I'm happy." Other sounds mean "I'm surprised" and "I'm delighted." There's also a sound for "You better give me that milk right away, I'm getting frustrated!" A baby accompanies each of his sounds with corresponding facial expressions, body postures, and ways of using his arms and legs. His communication is becoming purposeful, and he is using sounds as the centerpiece for getting the message across.

John Holt captures the purposeful nature of early babbling:

The baby who begins to talk, long before he makes any sounds that we hear as words, has learned from sharp observation that the sounds that bigger people make with their mouths affect the other things they do. *Their talk makes things happen.* He may not know exactly what, or how. But he wants to be a part of that talking group of bigger people, wants to make things happen with *his* voice [author's italics].

Why is the act of making sounds at the center of a baby's communication? After all, he has other ways of communicating such as pointing or making faces. In part it is because the human tongue is an extremely skillful and expressive muscle. Large areas of the brain are devoted to tongue movement and the interpretation of sensation from the tongue. Babies' tongues, and their ability to make sounds, are well developed very early in life—and will develop further during the period from eight to ten months through twenty-four months.

Orchestrating Sounds and Gestures

As baby Anna's repertoire of sounds demonstrates, humans quickly become very good communicators. Preverbal communication—communication without words—develops early and is well in place after six to eight months of life. This language of gesture, facial expression, and "nonsense" syllables develops until around eighteen months, when a child's words come in more and more. Of course, for many children, words have begun before that.

Getting the message across will become a more purposeful activity toward the end of the first year. From three months to around twelve months, a baby begins to bring together the sounds he can make with hand and arm gestures and body postures. He learns to coordinate all these skills. In addition, from eight months up to about age eighteen months, the baby (now an emerging child) begins interacting and communicating in patterns. At eighteen months, Jack takes his mother by the hand and walks to the bookshelf to show her the picture book he wants her to read to him. He takes Daddy to find a toy and points, grimaces, and makes sounds to tell Daddy to pick him up so he can reach it. Jack's sounds and the patterns they make, as well as his physical gestures, take on a larger meaning. He has a game plan in mind. He has begun to see the world in patterns, and he's making sounds in patterns as well.

At eighteen months, Jack uses his own private language. His parents can hear him speaking it to himself in his bed in the early morning before they go in to get him up. He babbles to them with this private language when they come in to say good morning. They know Jack's talking to them—in fact, he's talking up a storm even though it's not clear exactly what he's saying. Jack's parents enjoy their early-morning "conversation" with their son. As he babbles, they gesture to him, point at things in his room, and ask him questions to get a sense of what he means.

If you videotaped Jack's parents with their little boy, you would see that they are repeatedly exchanging signals with Jack, responding back to him so that there are from fifty to sixty circles of communication using a variety of gestures and sounds. That's a lot of practice in reading Jack's signals, and a lot of practice for Jack making sounds and patterns—accompanied by giggles, smiles, nuzzles, hugs—and they have a grand time together as they play.

Some families take a different approach, however, and discourage children's babbling. They expect kids to be quiet, to be "seen but not heard," not to bother anyone. Parents who insist on quiet children will have quiet houses. But they are unlikely to raise great communicators. Remember, a young child's babbling and private language lay the foundation for learning to use words effectively.

If you want to raise kids who are outgoing and assertive and confident in their ability to let you know what they want, you need to respond to and encourage all their gestures and sounds. Encouraging these preverbal elements of language by engaging in long exchanges and preverbal conversations will allow your child to think more and more in patterns. That is a critical step forward toward expressive language and complex communication. Celebrate it!

One mother told me a story about her second son, who was slower to talk than his older brother had been. He communicated effectively with gestures and facial expressions, letting her know what he liked to eat, which toys he wanted to play with, when he was upset with his brother, and so on. He was a big hugger and he used those hugs to show how much he enjoyed his family. But she worried that he wasn't using words. Just before she took him to see a speech pathologist for testing, he came up behind her one day, threw his arms around her knees, and held on tight. "I love you," he said. She canceled the appointment with the speech specialist. "Now we can't get him to shut up," she says of her son.

Later, when your children have leaned to use words fluently, they still communicate nonverbally. Your second-grader may smile and say, "Yes, I like to talk with my teacher," and yet his facial expression of annoyance and disgust says, "Get me out of here!" Communication is complex; a nonverbal message and a verbal statement don't always communicate the same things, and they may even contradict each other, as this second-grader's grimace shows.

Meaning and Desire

Before we communicate, we need to know what we want to say. But how does that happen? Unless we are planning to ask for a raise, propose marriage, or make a convincing argument, we don't stop and think to ourselves, "I'm going to say this or that." And even in those situations, our words don't always come out the way we had planned, even if we rehearsed them out loud.

Verbal communication comes out automatically; it just sort of flows. When we get into a conversation or debate, we are often surprised by what we hear ourselves say. We are thinking as we are talking. This process is so fast that we would be hardpressed to think through and plan every word we use. If we did that, verbal communication would be a slow, arduous task—as it can be for some people.

We invest our gestures—pointing, looking, showing—and our words or symbols with our feelings and our desires. It is that investment of intention that gives our words and gestures meaning and keeps us wanting to communicate.

When Kelly and her mother went shopping for a Halloween costume last fall, the preschooler didn't show much interest in the princess and ballerina costumes. But when they found a soft, fleecy sheepdog costume, Kelly said, "I *have* to have that one. I want to be a dog!" Her mom says that Kelly's little hands reached for the package and she clutched it to her chest. Her voice was filled with longing when she said, again, "I have to have this one."

Kelly's desire communicated itself so powerfully that for her mom there was no resisting her daughter's wish. And when Kelly wore the dog costume, she was ecstatic. You can see the joy in her face in the Halloween pictures. "I'm still not sure why the dog was so important to her," her mom says. "We don't have a dog, or even know any dogs very well. But maybe we should get to know some."

A child knows from his own feelings inside that he wants something. When a toddler sees juice, he realizes that he's thirsty. He wants juice! That wish finds expression when he matches the word "juice" with what he wants and says, "Juice, please" or "Want juice." If he didn't have that feeling, there would be no meaning to the word. He might see a picture of juice and say the word "juice" in a rote way. Or he might, again, repeat a television ad he heard just to say something to fill the air. But that wouldn't be meaningful communication. The meaning comes from having something to say. Having something to say always, *always,* relates to some wish, desire, or intent. The desire could be to share information. Every parent knows the feeling of listening to a torrent of reporting from an excited fourth grader about how the Egyptians built the pyramids, or of an outraged high schooler who has been reading about the civil rights marches in history class.

Stevie is fascinated by flowers and says, "Mommy, look at the yellow flower! Isn't that beautiful?" or "Mommy, I love that smell!" In the parking lot at school, Katie may say, "Daddy, can we have a big car like that someday?" when she sees a friend's family's brand-new SUV. Even "Hey, did you see that TV show last night?" is a question fueled by desire.

When Stevie says, "Hey, look at that yellow flower!" what is his desire? He wants his mother to understand his excitement, appreciate his curiosity, and share his delight in his observations. That's why we make comments, whether it's "Look how cute the cat looks asleep in that empty box" or "I'm so glad you came to this party with me. I don't know anybody else!"

When we're hanging out and telling a joke to a friend, or even when we are teasing somebody, there is desire involved. We might want to put someone else down to make ourselves feel better; that's why we tease. When your son shares a joke with a friend, he wants to share laughter and show that he's a cool, funny guy. Desire is even behind answering a question in school: A student responds to the teacher's questions to show that he knows the answers.

Desire, motivation, and emotion give words meaning and are just as much a part of taking in information as they are in conveying it. We also understand what other people are telling us through our emotions. We refer to our experience to interpret what they mean.

A mother says, "Do you want a cracker, sweetheart?" to two-year-old Susie, who has just learned the word "cracker" and the word "want." How does the little girl know what "want a cracker" means? She knows it because mother and daughter have been negotiating with gestures and words around crackers since Susie was eight months old. Susie has been pointing to the crackers, smiling when Mommy gives her one and says, "Here's a cracker." So when Mommy says, "Do you want a cracker?" with words, Susie know exactly what it means. If Mommy says, "Sweetheart, I love you," Susie knows exactly what that means, too. Why? Because Mommy has always hugged her and kissed her and played with her. Since the word "love" is associated with her enjoyment of these hugs and kisses, Susie already knows all about the word.

The Transforming Moment: Getting to Words

Sometime in the second year, children learn to communicate
with more than babbling, with a couple of words or short
phrases here and there, and with lots of gestures. By twenty-four
to thirty months, they use full sentences and begin having mini-
conversations with you.

I observed a two-year-old and her dad in the grocery store the
other day. Unlike many parents in the store, who looked ha-
rassed and were rushing to get their shopping done and be out
of there, this father was chatting with his daughter as they
wheeled though the aisles. They were in the canned fruit aisle,
and he was showing her pictures of fruit on the cans and asking
her whether she liked what was inside.

"Does Susannah like pineapple?" he asked, showing her
the can.

"Pine . . . app . . ." Susannah said uncertainly.

"Does Susannah like plums?" he asked.

"'Sannah like plums," she said.

Daddy placed the can in the cart and moved to the produce aisle.

"Does Susannah like cherries?" Daddy asked.

"I *like* cherries," the little girl shouted gleefully. A package
of cherries went into the cart.

"What about peaches?"

Susannah was on to the game now and decided to have
some fun with Daddy. "No peaches!" she said, and grimaced.

"Now, you're kidding me," her dad said. "I know you love
peaches." And he laughed.

Susannah laughed, too. "Love peaches," she agreed. Three
peaches went into the cart. Susannah clapped her hands.

What Susannah and her father were doing looked simple: having a playful conversation about fruit in the grocery store. But it represents a huge leap for Susannah, who is new to words. She has spent so much time babbling and gesturing with Daddy that she knows how to engage with him, how to communicate. Using her new-minted words and her budding sense of humor makes it a lot easier, a lot more fun—and also a lot more complex.

As we saw, emotions power the increasingly complex patterns that a twelve- to eighteen-month-old sees and understands. Jimmy sees Daddy's hat on the table. He wants to make Daddy laugh, so he points at the hat and makes clear his desire to grab it. Daddy picks it up and plops it on Jimmy's head, sending father and son into gales of laughter. Jimmy's desire, his wish to get the hat and make Daddy laugh, comes together with his new skills at making sounds and gestures. He gains his objective: the hat, and Daddy's laugh. Daddy completes the circle by putting the hat on himself and making a funny face at Jimmy. Jimmy expresses his pleasure with squeals and wiggles.

The more emotions a baby feels, the more variety he can put into his communication patterns. And the more his parents respond, the more they engage, the closer the baby moves to the next level: words!

How do babbling and gestures progress all of a sudden to using words, making sentences, and conversing almost like a little adult? To use words, to arrive at this marvelous transformation that separates human beings from many other members of the animal kingdom, a child has to learn to use symbols.

As discussed in *The First Idea,* the transformation happens when a child is able to do something very basic: separate perception from action. In other words, it happens when the child can separate what he sees—whether it is a picture of Mommy or Mommy in person—from automatically acting on it.

When a baby is young, much of what he sees is tied to direct action. He sees food; he reaches for it. He sees his mother; he pats her cheek. There's not much space between the perception and the action; they are tied together almost automatically. But when a baby or a toddler learns to interact through gestures and sounds, he can start a negotiation, such as pulling a parent to the kitchen table and pointing to the grapes he wants.

Reciprocal gesturing makes a link between seeing and action—between seeing the dish and reaching for it. These exchanges separate perception from action. And once you separate the two, you have something very new. In *The First Idea,* we call what happens at this stage the development of "freestanding perceptions or images."

What this means is that Susie can now see her mother but not be compelled to take immediate action. She has a picture of her mother in her mind—a picture that is invested with emotion, with desire. That picture begins to acquire all kinds of meaning. "Mommy" isn't just the person you grab or you cry with. Mommy can also be the person who plays with you. Mommy can be the person who comforts you. Mommy can be the person who tells you a funny story. Mommy can be the person who makes you giggle and laugh with a little tickle. Mommy can be the person who just makes you feel secure when she's in the room with you. All of a sudden, you can hold this freestanding image of Mommy in mind and, by attaching experiences to it, give it many, many emotional meanings. This is the birth of symbols.

Sound and Sense

During the second year of life, a child's ability to regulate his tongue, the muscles in his mouth, and his vocal chords grows and becomes more complex. This physical advance accompanies the intellectual advance a child makes during his exchanges of vocal signals and gestures with his parents. He is learning not only how to make a wide range of sounds but also how to hear and comprehend them. He is tuning his ears to hear and understand the language spoken around him and to him.

Here is where a family's specific spoken language becomes important, whether it is Spanish or English, Chinese or Swahili, French or Italian. As anyone who has ever studied a second language knows, each system emphasizes different sounds. As children hear a language spoken, they become better able to hear and make its particular sounds. As they learn to create symbols and match up sound patterns with those emerging symbols, they invest symbol and sound with meaning. The meaning comes from their emotional interactions with the people who talk with them over and over again—whether the word is mama, *maman,* or *madre.*

This remarkable confluence of events—symbol, freestanding image, and sound pattern—allows a child to relate to an image, say the word "mama," and know what it means. Sammy understands the word because he can discriminate its sound and invest it with meaning. By now, he has had a couple of years of emotional experience with his "mama." What an astonishing breakthrough this is!

Keeping the Conversation Going

As a child masters symbols and sounds, and can match patterns of these with meaning, he has language. He reached it through a series of big developmental steps and is ready to progress to still higher levels of communication. He will use his language in imaginative play and simple sentences; soon, he will begin to connect ideas together in a cause-and-effect way.

Now Sammy can tell his mother *why* he wants to go outside: "Because I saw Andrew out there." He can explain why he's sad: "Because you won't give me my bongo drum." He has complex ideas of his own and can understand complex ideas that are being expressed to him. When his mother says, "You can't play outside until I finish dressing and can keep an eye on you," he knows what she means—even though he may not like the answer.

Next, Sammy will be able to give multiple reasons for what he wants. "I want to go outside because Andrew has a basketball and needs me to play with him." When parents encourage conversation, asking their children "why" and "what" and "how," they will get richer, more complex answers.

One snowy afternoon I was sitting in a coffee shop next to a mother and her young son, who was probably in second or third grade. He was showing her all the things in his backpack, from two pieces of candy he got at a birthday party to a water-color painting he had worked on at school that day. As each item appeared, his mother asked him questions about it.

"Whose birthday was it today?"
"Jamal's. He sits next to me sometimes."
"Do you like Jamal?"
"Yeah, but I like Tony better."
"How come?"
"Tony always plays with me when we go out to the playground. Sometimes Jamal runs away," her son said.

Then he showed her his picture, which depicted a large boat filled with little figures.

"I like your picture," she said. "The boat looks pretty full."
"Yeah," her son said, "Everyone got on the boat."

"You draw lots of boats. Is this the same boat we have on the fridge?"

"Yeah, but this one has bigger waves!"

"We'll hang it up when we get home," his mom said.

His hot chocolate arrived, and the conversation slowed as he ate the whipped cream on top.

"Purple," he remarked, pointing to the paper napkin under his cup.

"Remember the purple plums we picked at Uncle Ivan's?" asked his mother.

"Yuck, they were sour!" the little boy shouted.

"Do you like bananas better?"

"Yes, with sprinkles!" her son chortled.

Their conversation goes on, even as they pack up and prepare to leave.

The comparisons and sense of humor between this mother and son suggest that they really enjoy talking together. This little boy will get lots of practice and become more and more expressive and verbal. His mother's questions were meaningful to him, evoking emotional connections with his friends, his artwork, and his taste in food.

As this boy grows older, his language will become more nuanced; he will not only compare and explain his feelings about Jamal and Tony but also tell his teacher several ways birds migrate, and say which is the most important, which second, and which third. He will understand and be able to explain degrees of things. His grasp of the gray areas of thought will make his language more elaborate and will move him closer to an adult level of communication.

Language and a Sense of Self

Once children can explain their own opinions and express why they prefer one activity or one person to another, they reach the stage I call "thinking off an internal sense of self." They can reach inside themselves for standards, values, and opinions to enrich discussions with others.

A mother told me about going to see her seventh-grade daughter present a project at school. Dana had read several books about the Underground Railroad and had done extensive research about the symbols escaping slaves used as they followed the trail to freedom. As her mother sat in the back of the classroom, Dana made a detailed and moving presentation about the road to freedom. She showed drawings she had made of the ways that escaping slaves used to communicate. She played a tape of the song "Follow the Drinking Gourd." But what amazed her mother was how eloquently Dana expressed herself as she spoke of what the slaves must have felt when they reached Canada and freedom.

"I was astonished at how grown-up she sounded," her mother said. "She seemed to be able to understand what the slaves were feeling and to be able to communicate it to us."

Dana's ability to imagine the feelings of others—even people quite unlike herself—came from her sense of her own values and her own ideas. She had deep feelings about the subject, and those feelings informed her presentation and made it eloquent and compelling.

The ability to judge communication against an internal standard also means that children can evaluate how they perform. In the classroom Johnny can say to his teacher, after he makes a flip remark, "No, that's not really what I wanted to say." Emily can realize, "When I recited that poem in class today, the words were just what I was feeling." Another classmate will say, "My essay was lousy. I didn't really care about it, like I did the last one."

As children move into their early adolescent years, language becomes increasingly reflective and abstract. This means they can use language *about* language; they can express in words their opinions and ideas about their own style and that of others. They can evaluate and respond to the opinions and arguments of others, whether it's a quiet talk about college options with a parent during a car trip, a sudden, harsh argument with a girl-friend, or a spirited debate with a history teacher.

As we said earlier, to be a good communicator, speaker, or writer, one has to have something to say! To be persuasive or moving on any subject, children, adolescents, and adults must have emotional interests in a variety of areas and be invested in thinking about them. The student talking to his dad about his college plans must have given some thought to what he might like to study and what kind of environment might be best for him. The boyfriend passionately arguing with his girlfriend must have developed an internal standard of how people in love are supposed to treat one another. The history debater must have delved eagerly into books about the early days of the Re-public or the role of the drafter of the Constitution, and so on. In each situation, the adolescent cares about what he has to say; he has an emotional and an intellectual investment that powers his ability to think and to shape language, tone, and gesture to get his message across.

By this point in children's lives, their higher levels of thinking and communicating are two sides of the same coin. So parents who hope to help children develop great communication skills need to help with thinking skills and to encourage opinions

about a wide range of subjects. If we teach children to memo-
rize facts from books or just parrot what we have told them,
they won't have a lot to say. If we solicit their opinions—"What
do you think about this? What seems to be wrong about my
argument?"—and listen to their answers, the nature of our conversations with them becomes more complex. And, of course,
we have to honor the sophistication and subtlety of their thinking and their language with complex thinking and expression of
our own.

A great communicator also has to be a great listener. In those
lawyerly debates about curfews, or dinner table political discussions, it is important that your child understands and acknowl-
edges your point of view. Such debates help kids learn to think
on their feet.

Some children and young people are quiet thinkers, not debaters, and parents need to recognize and honor this. Angela, a
tenth-grader, is shy about telling people—even family members—how she feels. But the poems she wrote for her school
magazine reveal a sensitive and thoughtful young woman.
When her poems were published, her parents celebrated by giving Angela a beautiful bound book of handmade paper to use as
a journal. They encourage her expressive writing by taking her
to readings and book signings and making sure that they ask to
see her recent work.

The skills that these quiet thinkers use are the same as those
the more vocal child uses: Listening, thinking, and communicating are all wrapped up in one. Quiet communicators may be
able to write a wonderful essay or an expressive letter, but they
find articulating themselves out loud a challenge. When parents ask such a child if they may read what he has written,
they're likely to find out a lot about what the child has been
thinking.

ENCOURAGING
GREAT COMMUNICATION

There are lots of recipes you can follow as you help your child become a great explainer and listener. But they all boil down to one essential ingredient: your willingness to engage him frequently in long conversations.

Communication between you and your baby gets under way in the first few weeks of life. When you respond to your infant's cries and agitated body movements with a sympathetic, soothing tone in your voice and a gentle expression on your face, he feels understood. Even at this early stage, you're providing him with valuable expectations of a response. In later months, as he begins to gain more control over his muscles and can arch his back or raise his head to connect with you, be sure to accompany your approving words with animated gestures that let him know you're reading him loud and clear. In fact, responding with empathetic gestures to those proffered by your preverbal child is even more important than using words.

By the time he's eighteen months old, you'll be exchanging as many as thirty or forty of these gestures over a ten- or fifteen-minute period with your child. The key to opening and closing these circles of communication and keeping the exchange going is to help your child take the initiative. It's not real gestural communication if you tickle his tummy and he giggles, and then you tickle his armpit and he snorts, and then you tickle him again, ten times in a row. True two-way communication occurs only when each new circle is somewhat different from the prior circle.

So if you and your baby are snuggling on the couch and he grins up at you, flash him a smile in return. Try sticking out your tongue and see what happens next. You'll probably be led into a funny face contest accompanied by silly sounds. Keep in mind that play should be fueled by your toddler's inner desires rather than your own impulse to direct the show. Follow the lines of your child's pleasure, whether it's making funny noises, wandering aimlessly around the room, playing with a light switch, or even flushing a toilet. As you respond to your child's actions, you're conveying to him that you empathize with his intent; that in turn makes him ever more eager to communicate with you.

A toddler exploring his playroom may have many things to show and tell you, many projects that need your cooperation. Let's say he's building a block house but has run out of pieces. He knows there is a another bin of blocks in the closet. Let him lead you there so that he can name or point to what he wants. Follow up on his eager desires and you'll find yourself in an ongoing conversation of words and gestures.

This kind of shared problem solving becomes more refined as your child learns to use more spoken language by the third year of life. Let's say your two-and-a-half-year-old makes a beeline for his favorite dinosaur when you sit down to play. When he turns away for a moment, you might hide the dinosaur high up on a shelf. A puzzled look is likely to steal across his face, or he may ask, "Where is he?" You might ask, "Where did he go?" As your child searches the playroom, you might comment, "This dinosaur must be a mountain climber!"

At any stage, don't fall into the trap of thinking that the non-verbal cues—smiles, frowns, wiggles, pointing, slumped shoulders, etc.—exchanged by the two of you are simply a warm-up act that is pushed to the side when he's able to speak in simple sentences. We continue to rely on our ability to read these kinds of nonverbal cues accurately until the day we die. We trust our gut that the boss is about to deliver bad news when he suddenly can't meet our eyes, or that the politician's glad-handing is as phony as it feels. So never underestimate the importance of helping your child become fluent in "gesture" as he progresses up the developmental ladder.

Parents have endless chances to spin out conversations. Little hurdles, as long as they aren't overwhelmingly frustrating, often make children even more eager and more verbal in reaching the object of their desire. So go ahead and create little obstacle courses and treasure hunts, and let your child make suggestions for solving the puzzles. These kinds of challenges encourage your child to take the initiative to put what he wants into words, both essential building blocks in higher-level thinking skills.

Cooperative play with you or another child can help a child to read and respond confidently to what another person is doing, thinking, and saying, and to use his own ideas in relationship to the other person's gestures, thoughts, and spoken words. Pretend play with a three-, four-, or five-year-old is an especially good way to encourage new ideas and connect them logically. If you should see your child nestle a stuffed animal or doll in his arms, for example, this can be the first act of an elaborate play in which characters get lost, are rescued, fed, and protected.

Let your child be the director, but play your part by enthusiastically entering the drama. When you're offered some pretend soup, you might be a little obstreperous and announce, "No, No, No! I want a cookie! No yucky soup!" If your "mommy" decides to take you to the store to buy you a box of cookies, announce that the car has broken down, or that you have to saddle the horse. In this way, you challenge your child to incorporate new ideas into your shared drama. Both his logic and his imagination are stimulated when make-believe play really gets going. As children approach school age, many will enjoy getting together to put on little plays, costumes and all.

In grade school, conversations may sound more like monologues than dialogues: "Oh, Dad, you wouldn't believe how unfair the umpire was at our soccer game. He kept calling penalties on us and looking the other way when their team was off-sides. It was so unfair!"

While your son catches his breath, you might say something along the lines of "I know just how you feel. That reminds me of the time when I was your age and the umpire didn't even blink when a kid elbowed me so hard in my chest that I fell down."

If your child plows right in with a non sequitur—such as "Why were you late picking me up after school, anyway?"—you've just been given an invitation to steer him back to more logical patterns of thinking: "But what about that umpire? How did the other kids feel?"

If your child repeatedly keeps on with a monologue, ask him to slow down and reply to your comments or questions. Help him become a more attentive listener. After all, a great kid is an interesting conversationalist, not a chatterbox. Of course, this also means being good listener yourself. Encourage your child's willingness to express his ideas by sometimes rephrasing what he has just said to let him know that you've been listening closely.

As your child approaches the middle school years, shared conversations can sometimes become lively debates. You might sometimes even deliberately be a little provocative. With a younger child, this can be gentle. With older teens, you might play the role of devil's advocate and challenge them to prove their points: "Wait a minute. What does having a seatbelt law have to do with civil liberties? Should people have the freedom to hurt themselves?" Or, "What if your school skipped some sports practice so there was more time to study?" Teenagers make brilliant debaters when the subject matters to them. By

challenging them now and then, you help them put their opinions into persuasive words.

Encourage your child to pick apart your own arguments. If
you show a little humility and ask in a genuinely nonthreatening way "So where did I go wrong?" we guarantee that she'll be
a more eager, active listener.

In all this, however, don't be dogged about an argument;
don't try to work in worthy lessons. It's the spontaneity and fun
that encourages their ideas and makes children want to hang
out and have long talks with you.

Helping Language Grow

1. With infants who are taking in the world: Vocalize with
   your baby; imitate their sounds repeatedly and match
   their rhythms.
2. With babies who are beginning to engage and relate: Talk
   to them, sing to them, let them hear sounds and see your
   facial expressions and gestures.
3. With toddlers: Learn to interpret your toddler's intentional
   pointing, sounds, and gestures; follow his lead and respond
   with words and actions.
4. When words begin: Celebrate your child's emerging words
   and repeat them back to him. Build on his natural interests.
   Ask him to tell you what he wants and help him get it.
5. With children who can talk in sentences: Let him be
   heard! Ask him to tell you stories. Engage in long conversations. Begin to ask "why" questions.
6. When logic begins: Keep asking those "why" questions and
   pursue the resulting conversation until you have reached a
   useful answer.

7. Complex dialogues: Ask for reasons, opinions, preferences. If a child says, "I want a new bike," ask for several reasons why. If he's upset with a friend, help him figure out why the fight happened. Encourage nuanced thinking by asking a child to explain all sides of the story.

8. Self-reflection: Ask your child's opinions about everything from politics to family dynamics. Listen carefully. Find out what he thinks about his own friendships, schoolwork, sports performances. Include your adolescent as an equal in adult conversations with yourselves and friends. Make sure he understands your point of view, listen to his, and respond so that he knows you hear him.

It's important to note that mustering a great argument doesn't mean a child can do what he wants to do. A lot of parents, unfortunately, confuse the two. They fear that if they create great communicators and great thinkers, the kids will get out of control. Not so. The better communicators and thinkers children are, the more they feel they have been heard and the better their judgment will become—and the more likely they will be to listen to your judgment. You, as parents, are not only entitled but also obligated to pull rank and exercise good judgment and good guidance for your children. But have that debate first before you exercise your guidance; your child is developing an essential skill to take with him into adulthood. He will be able to explain his feelings to his chosen partner; he will be able to talk to his boss about why he deserves a raise or a new responsibility; and he will be able to ask his children the same kinds of why questions you asked him. He will be able to tell his story.

5

Emotional Range
Passion and Balance

....

I watched a little girl, probably about four years old, as she waited for the Fourth of July parade to roll past on the street of her small town. She knew that some of the people in the fire trucks and antique automobiles and summer camp floats would be flinging candy out to the onlookers, and she was excited.

"Yay, yay, yay," she yelled when she say the first headlights of a fire engine approaching. "The parade's here, the parade's here!"

Her parents and the other people in her group laughed at her glee. Her older brother encouraged her, saying, "Astrid, tell them to throw the candy over here."

"Over here, over here," Astrid yelled, jumping up and down as the parade approached.

The firefighters on the first truck threw some Tootsie Pops onto the pavement. Astrid dove for them.

"Lollipops!" she exclaimed, as if she'd never seen candy before.

Now, any of you who have four-year-olds can imagine where this story is going. As the parade went by, Astrid became more and more wound up. When the last 4-H Club kids had walked by with their prize-winning calves, Astrid threw herself into her mother's lap in floods of passionate tears.

"It's *over*," she sobbed.

For one sunny hour, this little girl had experienced quite a full gamut of emotions: excitement and anticipation, laughter and joy, satisfaction and glee, and finally disappointment and sadness. Astrid did not cry for long after the parade went by. Her mother and father had remained calm throughout the parade, chuckling at her antics but not encouraging them. When she cried at the end, they patted her warmly and did not ridicule her for her tears. As her crying subsided, they suggested walking down the road for ice cream before they headed home. Calm now, Astrid took her mom's hand and walked off toward the ice cream stand.

BALANCING EMOTION

Children need to experience and express the full range of human emotions, from joy to anger to sadness. But *simply being able to express a range of feelings isn't enough: Children need to master the skill of returning to a sense of equilibrium,* as Astrid did with her parents' help.

For children, learning to find this emotionally secure place, an inner calm they can hang on to even in times of adversity, is a monumental learning task. It requires finding ways to comfort themselves and to bounce back from life's upsets. Emotional balance means staying cool under stress and remaining calm and focused in moments of crisis. To promote this balance, we need to allow our children to express their full range of emotions while encouraging them to do so in a calm and regulated way; we also need to offer appropriate discipline, guidance, and comfort as needed.

Understanding emotional range—recognizing the enormous variety of our emotions, whether it's the slight disappointment of missing a phone call from a friend, the joy of a family wedding, or grief over the death of a beloved pet—is not easy and takes lots of practice. But this understanding is critical to achieving balance. We need to be able to calm ourselves down when annoyed or angry, to feel and move through grief, to embrace joy. Being able to recognize our feelings and not be overwhelmed by them is an important developmental milestone. Practice for it begins in infancy as a baby learns how to calm herself so that she can attend to the world around her.

A Well-Balanced Person

When we say that a child or adult is "well-balanced," we usually think of an individual who has a rich spectrum of emotions, but also someone who can regulate those emotions.

Take Charles Jones, for example. He is an individual who can be assertive and creative and effective when leading others at work. He can enjoy playing golf or tennis and the feeling of competition. But he also can be enormously tender with his wife and empathetic and intimate with his children. He can understand how they feel.

When people threaten Charles because they disagree with him or because they want to put him down, he can sense what they are doing. Instead of feeling outraged and vindictive and wanting to squelch them in return, he feels mildly annoyed. But because he's also curious about why they are doing what they are doing, he is able to suspend his annoyance and think about the bigger picture that includes his own goals. Does he want to get into a pitched battle right now? Or does he want to encourage his detractors to cooperate with him? Is it worth working through their challenges or hostilities? Charles has the ability to make choices. Either he can assert himself and enjoy leadership or he can step back and leave the battle for another day.

Like all of us, Charles sometimes faces hardships. Recently, his parents were ill and he was very worried. When his mother died, he experienced a sense of deep loss and sadness—but it did not overwhelm him. Whenever he thinks about his mother, he experiences that sadness and sorrow again; yet he also has fond memories of her that make him smile or even laugh out loud. Charles is also anxious and worried about his father, who is mourning his wife and whose health continues to fail. He worries because he knows he will miss him terribly if he, too, should pass away. He wants his father to remain part of his own children's lives because he recognizes the importance of having a grandfather. Sometimes Charles is fearful for his own children. Will they grow up in a safe world? So many terrible things have happened that it is sometimes hard to remain optimistic about their future. But he does not let these worries interfere with his pleasure in being with them.

Charles embraces the full range of life's experiences and the emotions they produce—happiness, joy, intimacy, empathy, assertiveness, curiosity, anger, sadness, disappointment, anxiety. There is no area that he avoids or ignores or denies.

When Charles's kids don't listen to him and he has to raise his voice a little or create sanctions so that they will follow the guidance that he's providing, he gets annoyed and frustrated, as all parents do. But it's rare for him to lose his temper and yell. He is able to calm himself down for the most part and calm his children down if they are in the midst of a battle with him. He

is able to help his kids remain focused on what the real difference of opinion is about. Even if his kids cry and complain, he
knows that when he has to set limits, what he's doing is healthy.
His kids need his firm guidance to grow in a healthy way—and
he can be firm. They may be grumpy, or refuse to talk to him
for a few minutes because they are annoyed that he insisted they
turn off the television and do their homework, but Charles tol-
erates their annoyance and anger. He stays calm and collected
and regulated as he provides gentle guidance.

When Charles does lose his temper briefly—and after all, he's
only human—he regroups. If he feels he's lost it, he may even
apologize to his wife or his children and thoughtfully revisit
what led up to the point where they all lost their equilibrium. In
this way, Charles's emotional balance allows him to strengthen
his relationships even in times of conflict or stress.

Our Imperfect Nature

Lots of children and adults don't show emotional range and balance. Adults may have a hard time experiencing the full depth of
intimacy with loved ones. They may experience a connection,
even some warmth and some pleasure, but it's not that deep
sense of intimacy and pleasure that is possible in a close relationship. There are adults who can experience a little bit of annoyance but have trouble allowing themselves to give in to full anger,
even when they are frustrated, even when other people are doing
their best to make them angry. Other adults have difficulty with
feelings of sadness and loss. As soon as they are disappointed, or
as soon as things don't go their way, they get depressed. They feel
helpless and grow very anxious and worried.

We all know adults who have some of these limitations, sometimes on the side of assertiveness and anger, sometimes on the

side of intimacy and empathy, and sometimes on the side of fear
and worries. Instead of being able to tolerate these feelings, they
feel depressed or deny those feeling altogether, or become anxious without knowing why. And we, too, all have some restric-
tions in our emotional range, because, of course, to be human is
to be imperfect. If we try to achieve "perfection" in our emotions
or in how we control them, we become machine-like and lose the
spontaneous, vibrant nature of human emotion. We have to for-
give ourselves for our failings, even as we strive to live fully and
remain balanced.

Emotions and Balance in Infancy

A new baby experiences a huge rush of sensory experiences. To
make sense of these, she needs to learn to be calm and regulated
and not overwhelmed. All her senses—vision, hearing, touch,
taste, movement—are involved. Parents learn to recognize quickly
that even though they can't tell us about them, babies experience a
range of feelings—exuberance, frustration, happiness, joy, assertiveness, even a little bit of sadness. Parents encourage this
range not only by sharing attention with the child in different
emotional states but also by using all the child's sensations—sight,
sound, and movement—to do that. Lifting your baby high into
the air and laughing with her before you put her in her car seat for
a ride encourages her joy. Quietly patting her and cuddling her
when she seems sad or scared helps her learn to manage those feelings and regain calm.

We have said before that babies fall in love with us, their first
caregivers. This typically happens between two and four months.
Falling in love, of course, means warmth and connection. But it
can also bring frustration and anger as well as assertiveness and

curiosity. This first, loving relationship embraces a full dialogue of emotions, just as two adults experience all kinds of feelings together while still maintaining their love.

Communicating and Regulating Emotion

From infancy, children learn to convey the pain or euphoria they feel with those around them. They share their feelings, good and bad. They get the message to you through gestures. If your baby is angry because you're going off to work, she turns her head away when you reach down for a good-bye kiss. If she's delighted that you're taking her outdoors to play, she expresses it by clapping her hands. Toddlers can signal all the different emotions—assertiveness, joy, happiness—as well as sadness, disappointment, and frustration. These skills continue to develop.

Early in this chapter, we saw how four-year-old Astrid used her burgeoning communication skills to show how she was feeling. She jumped up and down, danced with glee, and pumped her fists in triumph when candy landed at her feet. She laughed and shouted and yelled when her brother encouraged her. She sobbed and hid her head at the end of the parade. She communicated.

As they grow older, children learn ways to increase or modulate a central emotion. A child can add to her delight by initiating and sustaining a fun game with a caregiver or another child; she can cope with frustration by learning to be patient and to take turns; she can tame her anger by learning to express it and then make up with a parent or a friend.

As children move into the stage of pretend play, their emotional repertoire and ability to regulate their emotions expand. They can use dolls and toys to experiment with feelings and find out how others react to them. Their make-believe games play out a range of human dramas and high-stakes emotion. With toys they express assertiveness, fears, caring, and empathy. Two little boys playing with trucks and animals might act out a car crash—and then set up a hospital where the hurt, frightened stuffed toys are quickly cured by caring doctors. Through this sort of play, children learn to keep fears and strong feelings under control. The psychoanalyst Erik Erikson pointed out that, for children, "mastering toy things becomes associated with the mastery of the [traumatic experiences] which were projected on them." In this way, children can test out all kinds of anxiety-producing feelings.

Parents can also get in the act. We can stir the imaginative juices of our children to explore play involving different emotional themes. We can help them stay in balance by guiding the interaction and not allowing the emotions to become too extreme.

Emotional Balance and Reflective Thinking

When children reach higher levels of logic and reflective thinking, they can draw cause-and-effect conclusions by talking about their emotions and beginning to analyze them. "Mary ignored me on the playground, so I feel angry, and sad, too." They can also see alternative conclusions: "Maybe Mary didn't see me; maybe she didn't mean to ignore me"; or "Mary looked as if she was having an argument with Andrea. Maybe she was too busy and upset to say hi to me at the same time." Seeing these nuances and being able to explain feelings to themselves helps children understand their emotions and bring themselves back into balance. This skill will be tested during the coming storms of adolescence; its mastery will serve our children throughout their lives.

ENCOURAGING
PASSION AND BALANCE

Helping your child become an emotionally vibrant, fully expressive person who is quickly able to return to a sense of inner calm after being stressed is a tall order. We all know adults who are comfortable about demonstrating caring, loving feelings but are hesitant to acknowledge their own aggressive impulses, or who quickly become enraged and have a hard time calming down. But since young children are very malleable emotionally, there are things you can do to facilitate their comfort with the whole gamut of human emotions—love, joy, sorrow, frustration, anger, aggression, competition, and shame. Even more significantly, you can give them the tools to center themselves when they're beset by strong feelings; these tools will enable them eventually to check impulsive behaviors.

Three important points should be kept in mind when helping infants, children, and adolescents to achieve emotional range and balance. It is extremely important, first of all, not only for parents but for all caregivers—educators, helpers, friends—to be very accepting of the overt expression of every kind of emotion. Also, make sure that the child's other caregivers allow this. Don't assume that certain emotions are good and other emotions are bad. This is how difficulties are set up in the beginning. If you assume that a child should remain compliant and sweet at all times and never show assertiveness or anger, she may either become impulsively angry or be very passive and cautious. Similarly, if we have the idea that children shouldn't ever cry, become upset, or be scared or worried, we may only cause them more fear and anxiety or make them less able to resolve their fears and anxieties. If we feel that children should never show their neediness or their dependency and always be self-sufficient, we may quash important components of intimacy and make children excessively needy or else lead them to deny their neediness and be falsely independent.

When a toddler experiments with assertiveness, enjoy that assertive interaction and work with it. If a child starts to climb on a wobbly chair to reach a toy up on the shelf, instead of saying, "No!" or "Get down right now!" stand near her and ask her what she wants. See whether she can signal to you with gestures that she wants the toy. Then either offer to hold the chair or pick her up to reach for the toy. That way, you make assertiveness a joint effort, a safe effort, a collaborative effort, not one that is squashed.

Second, it's important always to provide structure and guidance and limits so the child doesn't become overwhelmed by her emotions. Engage the child in a way that is regulated and guided and has inherent limits. When a child wants to walk at the edge of a pond, help her do it in a safe and secure way. If the child is trying to do something that is dangerous, we set a limit—even if it means that the child will be temporarily annoyed and frustrated. This helps the child realize that she can't do everything she wants when she wants—that is, we help her begin to regulate her emotions and tolerate some frustration.

For caregivers, engaging in an emotion means accepting it, interacting around it, and negotiating with it, but it does include limits. Let's say your child wants a hug. You engage her in the hug; you interact; you exchange a lot of joyful sounds and squeezes. But let's say your daughter continually wants to hug while you're on the phone with Grandma. She's becoming a nuisance and wants all the attention. That's when you may have to hold her in your lap and say, "Shhh, shhh." You may have to help her sit next to you and hold your hand quietly while you are talking to Grandma on the phone.

What you are doing here is setting limits, guiding and regulating, all around that same emotion of joyful closeness and intimacy. Find a compromise where the child is close to you but is also setting limits on her own exuberance. You're accepting her feelings and engaging with her, but through your calm firmness you're regulating her behavior at the same time. We call this process "counter-regulating."

A third important way to help your child experience a full range of emotions without being overpowered by them is to know your child's individual differences and also your own. Some children are highly sensitive to sound or touch. To such a child, the more assertive, aggressive, or competitive side of life will be scary because she is overwhelmed by loud, assertive voices or by too much roughhousing and touching. The child who is under-reactive to touch or sound may crave these same kinds of experiences. But she may have a harder time experiencing sadness or frustration without feeling aggressive and, therefore, without getting out of control or impulsive. Similarly, an over-sensitive child may have trouble with fears or anxieties because they tend to overwhelm her.

You have to know your child's temperament if you want to broaden her emotional range gradually in a safe and secure way. A very sensitive child may not want to play a rough-and-tumble game right away, but may want to play a gentle pat-a-cake game. After some months, that gentle play may lead to a little arm wrestling or another kind of game that gets more assertive. On the other hand, your rough-and-tumble child, who craves sensory input all the time, may have a harder time with relaxing and learning about empathy and closeness and intimacy. You may have to introduce these gradually, first running together with the child while holding hands, then jumping together, and then maybe some engaging in rhythmic activity that becomes a little quieter and quieter and quieter until you are, at the end of the day, just lying on the floor together giving each other back rubs and experiencing that gentler closeness.

Each child needs to be drawn into the full range of emotions through his or her own window of individual differences. But your own sensory patterns matter as well. If you are highly sensitive to noise and commotion, you'll have a harder time encouraging assertiveness. If you are highly physical and active, you may have a harder time with certain elements of empathy or intimacy. You may not have differences in the way you actually process sensations, but you may have differences based on how you were brought up. So you need to ask yourself whether there were certain emotions you avoided because of sensitivity, or that were downplayed or constantly encouraged when you were growing up. By respecting your child's and your own feelings, the two of you can negotiate a greater and greater emotional range and a better and better balance.

The process of working with your child's individual differences begins when an infant is lying in your arms or gazing at you from her changing table; you can pay special attention to those times when she seems agitated or unhappy. After you've ruled out obvious stressors such as a dirty diaper or a colicky tummy, see how you can adjust her environment to help her calm herself. Perhaps she's sensitive to bright lights (turn off the overhead light and switch on a bedside lamp instead) or high-pitched noises (speak in a softer, lower tone; hum instead of singing to her). If she seems somewhat unresponsive to sights or sounds, put a gleam in your eye, speak with more animation, and enthusiastically raise your eyebrows when you gaze at her. If you've observed that she whips her little arms and legs back and forth as she cries, try swaddling her in a receiving blanket—many infants seem less distracted when their limbs aren't "lost in space."

Continue to pay attention to your child's sensory system as she becomes more mobile. Most toddlers enjoy movement in space, and they love it when you push them on a swing. But you'll soon notice whether your two-year-old prefers being pushed hard or gently, and what kind of swing makes her feel secure. Some children can experience the heady joy of flying through space only when they feel regulated by firm pressure on their backs. An enveloping spandex swing may be just the ticket.

In adapting to a child's special way of reacting, you can also expand her range. If your toddler is a reticent explorer, challenge her to be more assertive very, very gradually. Don't rush in and try to "make" her have more gumption. Instead, try devising a game that with a little help from you will exploit her own natural interests. Why not put a brand-new slinky high up on a countertop so that your child is motivated to reach it by climbing up the mountain of pillows and cushions that the two of you have constructed?

Throughout childhood, it is important not to inhibit appropriate expressions of emotion. When your child experiences disappointment or annoyance, help her find ways to express these feelings with empathetic gestures and words of your own.

Pretend play enables a verbal child to try on various emotions for size. But not infrequently you'll notice that she avoids toys or taking on roles that relate to symbols of power or aggression (witches, wizards, monsters, and the like), yet is very comfortable, on the other hand, launching happy teddy bear parties. You might then ask, "How come our teddy bears are always hugging each other?" Although you're letting the child lead off with the emotional themes that she feels comfortable exploring, you can introduce a rambunctious teddy into the drama that will not only deepen the plot but expose your child to emotions that she's previously avoided.

Welcome hearing about your child's aggressive, jealous, or competitive thoughts during pretend play—even if you have issues with expressing such thoughts yourself. Both of you can assume bad-guy roles from time to time, roaring like monsters or becoming wicked Captain Hook as he makes a Lost Boy walk the plank. This will reassure your child that no feelings are taboo and that all feelings have equal weight.

By experiencing negative emotions in a safe environment where she knows she will be understood and not judged, your child will learn to express these feelings—through gestures, conversations, and pretend play—without being overwhelmed. If she finds herself unable to forgo acting out her uncomfortable feelings and hurting herself or others, you have a chance to remind her that there's a difference between thinking, feeling, and talking about feelings, which is always acceptable, and taking them out on others, which is not. As you counter-regulate with extra soothing and comforting when meltdowns occur, your child will learn to internalize that soothing and gradually be able to incorporate it into her own emotional repertoire.

An older child can anticipate troublesome feelings in future situations. As you encourage her to imagine the feelings she's likely to have when she walks into her new school for the first time, or how her brother is going to feel when he finds out she's scratched his favorite compact disc, she'll be learning to accept, yet control, these feelings.

Should her sixteen-year-old brother see red when he spies his scratched CD, it's important to remember that he, too, shouldn't be chastised for feeling angry with his kid sister. When you hear his shout of dismay, try calming the situation by having your daughter apologize to her brother for taking the CD and then offering to buy a replacement. When your teenager continues to vent, raising his voice and pointing an angry finger at his sister, he, too, is experiencing a legitimate human emotion. As long as he keeps his behavior in check and doesn't start hitting his sister, you needn't inhibit him. Make sure there's no taboo on feelings. Great kids need to express themselves and learn to handle the whole gamut of human emotions.

Helping a Child Express and Balance Emotions

1. Figure out what helps a baby become calm and regulated, which sounds, sights, and movements are soothing.
2. Help a child learn to regulate emotions by becoming calmer yourself when a child is overexcited and by offering warmth and reassurance when she is sad and withdrawn.
3. Express and explain your own range of emotions as you interact with your child.
4. Allow assertiveness and anger as well as compliance and happy feelings.
5. Help a child become a poet of her feelings through pretend play and conversations about how she feels.
6. When a child is older, try play-acting games to enable her to anticipate future feelings.
7. Remind children often that no feelings are taboo.

As the world of the adolescent expands with new independence and a powerful sense of the approaching future, emotional seas can become stormy. Their bodies are changing, and powerful romantic and sexual feelings make life an emotional roller coaster. At the same time, independence requires more responsibility, at school and at home. All this can be a cause of celebration and excitement. But these physical changes and increasing emotional and intellectual demands can make it harder for teenagers to maintain internal (and external!) balance. This is a time when slammed doors, interrupted dinner conversations, and angry phone calls become familiar to parents. Fortunately, the teenage years also offer times of deep, intimate conversations about the meaning of life, values, justice, and other important topics. You may find that these conversations are easiest when you are doing things together and your teenager doesn't have to make eye contact with you. While cooking dinner or raking leaves, parents of teenagers have a chance to express affection and remind them that we love and admire them.

As adolescents range beyond the family, emotional balance becomes essential—in college, in the workplace, and in the larger society. To operate successfully at work, we have to be able to stay calm and regulated in the face of competition and frustration, as well as in times of success. Later, relationships with spouses and children bring a whole range of feelings—including loss, whether it is a toddler's first day of school or the death of our own parents.

Throughout our lives, we can learn to increase our emotional range and our ability to readjust our balance. We can move toward healthier and healthier patterns, and we can help our children do the same.

6

Genuine Self-Esteem
The Importance of Self-Awareness

....

Last summer, eight-year-old Annie signed up for a diving competition at her neighborhood pool and invited her mom and dad to watch the event. They watched as Annie, wearing a bright red tank suit and a white bathing cap, stuck to the low board for her dives.

But during the final round, Annie looked over at her parents, shrugged, and then resolutely walked over to the tower leading to the high board. Up she climbed. She walked to the edge, rose up on her toes—and dove! Her form wasn't exactly perfect, but when Annie emerged from the water she was grinning from ear to ear.

"I did it, I did it!" she crowed. "I knew I could do it."

Now, Annie didn't win a ribbon that day, and she probably won't ever train for the Olympics. But she went home feeling really good about herself and her performance.

"That was brave, going off the high board," her mom said as they drove home.

"Yeah," Annie said. And then repeated, almost to herself, "I *knew* I could do it."

Where did Annie gain the confidence to try something new in front of a crowd of people, including her mom and dad? Why did she feel so great afterwards? Because she is a self-aware, confident, and optimistic child. The smile Annie gave when she emerged from the pool—an expression that her mother recognized as the same ear-to-ear grin she started flashing at eight months—expressed her strong sense of self-esteem.

FOUNDATIONS OF SELF-ESTEEM

Self-esteem is a critical trait for all children, and for all adults. It is that fundamental sense of feeling good about who we are at our very core. Self-esteem also is something you hear about all the time, whether it's in parenting articles, on television, from your child's teachers, or in casual conversation with other parents. But developing this trait is not quite as simple as people make it sound.

Take Ethan, for example. All his life, Ethan was told that everything he did was terrific. His parents believed that praise was important and that they could create positive self-esteem in their son by applauding his every effort. The trouble was, their praise poured out no matter what. Ethan never knew whether he was really being good at something or just being praised whatever he did: "Oh, you're so wonderful . . . "

This unconsidered praise left Ethan feeling unsure. He went around seeking reassurance all the time. He would go to his friends with his homework, or his older sister with an art assignment, and anxiously ask, "Is this okay? Am I doing it right?" In class, he needed to keep going up to the teacher's desk to ask,

"Have I gotten it right this time?" Ethan never felt entirely sure of himself.

Then there's the other end of the spectrum. Sally grew up in a family where nothing she did was ever good enough. She always felt criticized. Her parents believed in tough love and kept pressing their daughter to do better. She felt she could never please them. Eventually, Sally took her parents' attitude to heart and said to herself, "Well, I can't do anything right. Whatever I try won't go well, so why try?" She was constantly negative about herself and was afflicted with a chronic low-level depression. She avoided trying new or difficult things at which she felt little hope of succeeding.

Neither one of these admittedly extreme parenting approaches produced a confident, self-accepting child, although both Ethan and Sally's parents thought that what they were doing was right. Ethan's parents made their son's life too easy; Sally's made her life too hard.

Just Enough Challenges

Self-esteem is not based on a constant bath of warm praise. Rather, it comes from the brisk refreshment of overcoming obstacles on your own—whether it's learning to open a cupboard door to reach the cookie jar or concentrating through the math portion of the SAT—allied with warm acknowledgment of your value from others. The more challenges you face and overcome as you grow up, and the more the people you care about notice those well-earned victories, the better you are likely to feel about yourself.

As my little story about Annie and the diving board illustrates, feeling good about yourself has to do with making progress. Annie made literal progress from the low to the high board. But how did she develop the self-confidence, indeed the courage, to take that step? Part of the reason is that her loving parents were wise enough to let her fail sometimes. They didn't do her homework for her, and sometimes she handed in careless work filled with spelling mistakes. But when she learned to take more care with her papers, the big red A on top was something she knew she had earned herself. Many experiences like these, coupled with hugs both when she was upset and when she was happy, set Annie on the path to the high board—to self-esteem and self-acceptance.

A child who is given everything, and is helped over every high fence in his way, may not have the basis for as much self-esteem as someone who has to take a deep breath and climb over on his own. A child who is thwarted by endless tasks and hurdles he can never overcome will also find it hard to feel good about himself. You know the old saying, "Getting there is half the fun." Well, when it comes to self-esteem and self-acceptance, getting there is all the fun.

Self-esteem involves many aspects of development. It has to do with developing an awareness of one's body—and feeling good about the body and what it can do. It has to do with basic attitudes about the world, with developing an optimistic, can-do attitude that pays off in a sense of pride and accomplishment. It has to do with recognizing strengths and weaknesses, and with learning the difference between them. It has to do with accepting one's weaknesses and being willing to work on them, yet at the same time taking pleasure and pride in one's strengths.

Self-esteem also has to do with self-image. It means being able to picture yourself and to view these pictures with positive feelings. Annie undoubtedly did this before she mounted that ladder to the high board; she imagined herself making the climb, performing the dive, and bursting out of the water brimming with success.

Self-esteem, as we have seen, requires realistic self-awareness. It means thinking about yourself and figuring out that you can feel good by tackling difficult things, figuring out effective strategies for getting there, and focusing your energies on areas that are important to you. Of course, children don't do this alone. At every stage, their parents and other adults should be in the trenches with them, coaching them to try something new, reassuring them that they can go a little farther, admonishing them when they give up too quickly, and praising them when they legitimately finish a task well and with their own individual flair.

As a human being grows, those tasks evolve from building sandcastles to jobs such as feeding the family dog or setting the breakfast table, then on to life-changing tasks such as trying out for a scholarship, completing a college essay, landing a first job, or deciding to start a family of one's own. At every stage, parents play a role, whether they are literally kneeling on the beach with their toddler and handing him a bucket, not-so-gently reminding their ten-year-old to refill the dog's water bowl, or being available to listen to an essay or role-play and stage a mock job interview. Even when our children are adults—indeed, even after we are gone—we remain in the trenches with them, challenging, celebrating, and comforting them with our attention, concern, and love. Our presence is central to their self-esteem, though it can be tricky to know when to jump in and help and when to stand aside, encourage, and cheer.

Our children's self-awareness—their ability to know and reflect about themselves—enables them to identify the kinds of relationships that will work for them, the areas of study that will bring them pride and pleasure, and the kind of work and leisure activities that will satisfy them. Ultimately, it involves forming core values and expectations of life and then formulating a strategy to achieve them. When children learn to internalize a set of values, know what to strive for, and can keep an eye trained on that path even as they judge their own progress, self-esteem and self-awareness reinforce each other.

First Lessons

Like all the other traits that define a great kid, self-esteem starts at the very beginning of the journey, in infancy. Joshua is his parents' first baby. Two accomplished professionals, they waited until they were well into their thirties to become parents. They adore their baby and find him miraculous. They are playful, comfortable with their tiny boy. Erica likes to pick Joshua up and sing to him when she wakes him from his nap. One afternoon, she stood a little bit away from his crib and sang a song she had loved as a child:

"Mares eat oats and does eat oats, and little lambs eat ivy," she sang, a bit off-key.

Joshua, who had been lying placidly on his back, turned his head toward the sound. His mother saw him turn, and stopped singing to greet him with a huge smile. Then she walked to the other side of the crib and started singing again.

"Mairzy dotes, and dozey doats," she sang in a funnier voice.

Joshua turned his head the other way—and there was Mommy, smiling at him again.

This ritual turned into a regular wake-up game for Joshua and his mother. To his parents' delight, Joshua's head-turnings graduated to joyful wiggles of his arms and legs, and to laughs and smiles of his own.

As Joshua looks, listens, and turns towards the sights and sounds in his world, he is beginning to develop a sense of mastery. He is beginning to recognize the world outside himself. When he turns his head and finds Mommy's face and sees her beaming back at him, he feels powerful. When she sings "Mairzy-Doats" and he wiggles in rhythm with her voice, he feels ever better.

Of course, Joshua doesn't experience those feelings in the same way an adult does, with conscious awareness, with thoughts. But he does experience them.

In the earliest stages of development, Joshua will continue to learn about the world and himself without the use of thought. Learning about his own body and his place in the world will lay the foundation for Joshua to function in a purposeful way as he grows older. In time, he will learn to regulate his basic functions such as eating and eliminating, and he will take pleasure in touch and movement. This sense of well-being in the body is fundamental to his self-esteem.

As adults, we also experience wordless feelings of self-regard and self-esteem. Sometimes, we just feel it in the core of our bodies, in the core of our being, as we gaze at someone we love or walk in the sun with a friend after recovering from an illness. This wordless joy is likely what a new baby feels. He's developing that core sense of being related to the world and feeling the pleasure of engaging with others. That feeling comes from things he's doing—looking, turning.

By turning his head to his mother's song, Joshua is able to take a little bit of control over how he feels. And right there is the key to self-esteem: He is *making something happen.* He is turning, he is looking, he is listening, he is smirking, he is smiling, he is frowning, he is moving. All these actions not only elicit responses from his parents but also give him a wordless sense that "I can do something!"

The key to developing this early sense of "can-do" is to couple the pleasure of connecting with an admiring, loving, joyful, and intimate adult with some act on the child's part that helps make it happen. The joy should not simply be handed to the child so that he becomes just a passive responder to a tickle or a hug. When he is actually trying—by turning, by looking, by listening—to find that wonderful, beaming face, he is learning his first lesson in self-esteem. And it's a glorious lesson.

John Holt, in *How Children Learn,* talks about the effects of the little games we play with babies:

> Recently Lisa (sixteen months) has started to play fierce games. She bares her teeth, growls, roars, rushes at me. I pretend to be afraid. It can go on for some time. From this and many other things she does, it seems that she feels a *me* inside her, growing stronger, doing things, demanding things. . . . [Games like these] give a child a stronger feeling of cause and effect, of one thing leading to another. Also, they help a child feel that he makes a difference, that he can have some effect on the world around him.

A sense of engagement, warmth, and delight in others is the foundation for self-esteem. After all, self-esteem means bringing inside yourself that glow of positive regard that we feel in our loving relationships. We can't have an inner voice, an inner sense that we are good people, without feeling that in our earliest relationships. It doesn't come out of the blue; it doesn't come from a genetic code. It comes from those early connections with warm and loving caregivers.

Some researchers suggest that certain people are genetically happier or more joyful than others. And there may be some people who are wired to smile a little bit more and some who may be more optimistic in their "hardwired" nature. But these basic qualities, which may have genetic components, don't automatically turn into self-esteem unless they are fueled by a loving relationship. A baby needs the warm glow of another being, the feeling of basking in the pride in another person's eyes as he accomplishes something for himself, even if it is as basic as looking and listening or a big smile.

By the end of the first year of life, this connectedness and sense of purpose expands as the baby learns to reach for a small toy perched on his father's head or to find a rattle hidden in his hand. These exchanges, too, lead to a glow of positive feeling, to self-esteem.

More elaborate problem solving follows in the second year of life. This, too, reinforces a child's self-awareness and self-esteem. As a toddler discovers a new toy Grandma has hidden near the sandbox, his pride and sense of accomplishment expand. The agenda becomes more complicated as the child's abilities grow.

During this stage, wise parents challenge their child just a quarter of a step beyond what he can do. There may be some frustration at first, but the child will soon find the solutions. When he stretches his ability, as he figures out how to stack blocks ever higher and higher, he realizes the payoff: shared joy and pride with his parents. By doing it with his parents, he feels their acceptance and pride; this is coupled with his own real effort and sense of internal mastery of a new skill.

This sense of mastery becomes part of the toddler's inner self-image. As Erik Erikson writes: "A child who has just found himself able to walk seems not only driven to repeat and perfect the act of walking . . . he also becomes aware of the new status and stature of 'one who can walk.'"

The Power of Ideas

In the third year of life, children can experience self-esteem not only at the level of basic feelings but also at the level of ideas. Now, a child can not only see his mother laugh when he hugs his teddy bear, he can picture her smiling at him *inside his own mind.* He can play that pleasure out with his bears by giving them "high fives" or making them hug each other.

With ideas, he can picture the kinds of things that delight him, the kinds of activities he wants to try. He can rehearse them in his own mind, and he can imagine solutions to problems without actually carrying them out. His thoughts become a source of pride and excitement. When he has an interesting idea, he can recognize its merits and feel proud.

How does a child learn to value his ideas? Once again, it happens in loving relationships. When parents get down on the floor and play with a child and give high fives to his stuffed bear, too, they show that they value his imaginative ideas. They show that his ideas are as important as his actions. A parent who is too busy does not encourage ideas. A parent who is always negative about what a child is doing and interrupts play because the child might break something or get dirty gives the child the impression that his activities and ideas are scary or worrisome. In these circumstances, the game he's playing won't bring pleasure and pride. Celebrating and entering into his games—not worrying that it makes you muddy or wet—shows the child that his invention has value, that *he* has value.

Your three-year-old's ability to hold you in mind when you are not there contributes to his self-esteem. When he's playing alone, he can picture you smiling at him and approving his accomplishment, whether it is completing a puzzle or stacking the blocks as high as they can go.

Logic and Self-Esteem

With the advent of logic, a child learns a new level of self-esteem and self-acceptance. He is beginning to see the world as a place of consequences: "If I'm a good boy, which means I eat my fish sticks and stay in my seat, I'll get a big smile from Mommy. She'll ruffle my hair and be happy with me. If I give her a hard time, Mommy will frown and be annoyed with me."

Logical thinking is a great boon to the child. It enables the child now to know just what will bring him praise and smiles from others and what will bring him the opposite. He can begin making deliberate choices about how to behave.

With this ability to anticipate consequences, a child has more control over his own internal self-esteem. Yet he doesn't always use the behavior he knows will make him feel good. To his mother's distress, he begins to give her a hard time. He's defiant and bratty. He throws his fish sticks on the floor and refuses to go to sleep at bedtime, even though he knows this behavior will upset his parents. What's more, he seems to enjoy teasing them.

Why do children do this when they are able to formulate the consequences of behaving badly? Although there are many reasons for a child to feel frustrated, parents can get into a pattern in which they do not challenge the child, do not give him something to strive for. Yet it is this extra effort that lets a child feel pride in a new accomplishment. If asked to help set the table, or given a fork to use instead of his fingers, or moved from his high chair into a booster seat at the grown-up table, he will have something new to feel good about.

Parents sometimes set the bar too low for their children. When a child is protected and indulged too much, he may feel frustrated. As a consequence, he may decide that "love by irritation," as my colleague Reginald Lourie used to call it, is better than being allowed to do and have whatever he wants. Over-indulgence may make him feel he is being taken for granted. He may then grow angry and feel neglected and deprived of the feelings of accomplishment and self-esteem that he intuitively desires. So he tries a different policy to gain attention—and drives his parents to distraction.

If this is what is happening, parents need to take a close look at the environment they are creating for their child. Are they gradually challenging the child to reach new skills and intellectual milestones and giving him a feeling of progress? Some fresh new challenges, from playing catch to learning to ride a bike, can move a child out of a negative cycle.

Even when challenged with interesting new tasks, as children move up the next rung of the ladder, feeling good about themselves becomes more complicated.

Jay lives in a row house in the city, but there is one cherry tree in the small backyard. Jay is forbidden to climb the tree, but he loves to look at it out of his bedroom window. In springtime, the tree is covered with beautiful, pale-pink blossoms.

Jay can't resist. One morning, while his mother is making his breakfast, the five-year-old heads outside and shinnies up the truck of the tree. Now, he understands very well that he's being mischievous. But he also knows that what he's doing is a little bit exciting and exploratory. He knows that his mother is going to be upset with him for climbing, especially since no one else is in the yard. But he also knows that she won't be able to resist smiling when he hands her the spray of blossoms he climbed up the tree to pick for her. Life, and Jay's perception of it, has become more nuanced and complex.

As a child learns to be a gray-area thinker, he develops a more finely tuned picture of himself. He recognizes that he is someone who behaves most of the time, but not all the time, someone who can do a good job in some things but has a harder time with other things. He is beginning to develop a more realistic sense of himself, and with it, a more complex kind of self-esteem.

Self-Esteem on the Playground

When children enter grade school, their sense of self-esteem becomes complicated by their individual roles in the group. Are they in or out, up or down? Are they chosen first for kickball, or last? Are they good students, or do they struggle? Do other kids like them? How much?

Parents know that these measurements of status and success in grade school change from day to day because our kids come home and give us detailed news bulletins about who picked whom as a playmate, who cried in class, or who got an A-plus on a test. For the kids living through what I call the "playground politics" stage, the changes can feel as if they were happening minute-to-minute. And even a child with a robust sense of self-esteem may feel buffeted by the changing alliances on the playground and the ever-increasing demands of the classroom.

In the shifting hierarchies of playground politics, children learn to compare themselves to other children. During the early school years, the largest source of self-esteem often comes from how children picture themselves in relationship with their peers. Though it comes often with pain, the ability to assess and evaluate how you stack up with peers is a great intellectual, emotional, and social accomplishment. A four-year-old can't do that!

Luckily for children going through this stage, they are also becoming ever more adept at seeing shades of gray. Ellen, a budding artist, begins to understand that she doesn't have to be the best at *everything*. She's not so good at kickball, but she's great at painting. Liam may not be much good at doing his math word problems, but he's a whiz at telling jokes and making the whole class—including his teacher—double up with laughter. Meanwhile, quiet Lucas burns through his math problems and asks for more difficult ones to try.

At this stage, children's hopes and dreams for themselves, their sense of their future, also come into play. You can't take pride in yourself without having wishes or aspirations against which to measure your accomplishments. If parents and teachers show children that they can constantly make progress and move toward greater mastery, their internal sense of can-do, and their sense of pride within the microcosm of a loving family, continues to grow, even as they discover their own limitations. On the other hand, a child can be the best baseball player, mathematician, or reader in the class and still feel very low self-esteem if the relationships at school and at home are judgmental, or if no one seems to care.

Tamara is a bright little girl who has a precocious verbal ability. The youngest child of a writer and an editor, she loved nothing more than making her parents glow with pride at her cleverness and wit. She started reading early, and she made up stories as soon as she could write.

But as school progressed, Tamara found out that she wasn't so good at a lot of other things. When she got her report cards, her mom and dad would zero in on the minuses (handwriting, sitting still in class, math) and no longer seemed to notice her strengths at all.

As she moved up from grade to grade in school, Tamara found that it was tougher and tougher to do her homework. When she faced a blank page, she seemed to freeze up. She might spend homework time arranging her dolls on their shelves or drawing pictures. (Her family had no television.) The homework went undone—although she meant to do it. She found herself telling her mom she didn't have any, or that she had done it at school. Then, when it was time to go to bed, Tamara would toss and turn and worry about the undone paper. She knew she would be in trouble at school the next day.

Tamara got pretty good at zipping through her assignments in the backseat of the school bus. She didn't do them well, but she did them. As she dashed off her work, though, she felt awful, as if her heart were too big for her chest. Sometimes she felt as though she couldn't really take a good, deep breath, the kind that fills your lungs up and makes you feel strong and refreshed.

What Tamara was feeling was the opposite of self-esteem. She was experiencing shame. And her shame paralyzed her. It got in the way of playing with her friends. It got in the way of her joy and silliness. It interrupted her sleep. And it sat right in the middle of her path to self-esteem.

But Tamara was lucky. Her teacher noticed what was happening and took time to coach Tamara in two important things: admitting when she couldn't do something and figuring out how to get her work done by breaking it up into smaller bits. As she started finishing her assignments, Tamara felt a lot better about herself. Her parents still focused on her failures more than her successes, but she felt she had an ally in her teacher, who reminded her of her strengths. And she discovered how to talk herself through when she got stuck. It worked more often than it didn't, and Tamara started to feel lighter and more carefree, even as she was doing more work at school.

As Tamara found out, the ability to size yourself up and be honest about your failings as well as your successes is an important step toward realistic self-esteem. But she needed the warmth and acceptance of an adult before she could face those weaknesses and be able to work on them.

"How Am I Doing?"

If children enter adolescence with a strong sense of their own strengths and weaknesses, and a healthy self-regard, the storms of adolescence are likely to be punctuated with periods of sun-shine and joy. Upon leaving middle school, with its elaborate pecking order and intense focus on the group, kids enter a world filled with more possibility for self-awareness and expression. A boy who has been defined as a great soccer player can try his hand at art projects without worrying about losing status. A girl who has been rejected by the cool crowd on the playground may find a new level of acceptance and success in the drama club.

In the adolescent years, great kids have a well-defined self-image and sense of self-awareness. They also become better at evaluating themselves and their thoughts, at recognizing their feelings, and at judging who they are. The key to such self-examination is the ability to judge oneself against an internal standard, an internal set of evolving values and goals, and an ideal vision of the kind of person you wish to be. These stan-dards are gradually formed by observing or reading about role models of all sorts—a teacher, an astronaut, a pediatrician, a tennis star, as well as aunts, uncles, and older siblings. Teenagers and young adults can have internal images of themselves as lov-ing, caring people, as empathetic people. They see themselves as striving to earn a place in a particular occupation or career.

As I said at the outset, being a "great kid" does not necessarily mean that your son will go to Yale or your daughter will become an astronaut. But a great kid will aspire to be a good person, whether that means a good person and an electrician, a good person and an elected official, a good person and a librarian, a good person who raises a family, or a good person who travels the world working for peace. Chapter Ten will delve more into the moral standards that mesh with career aspirations.

Remember how Mayor Ed Koch of New York used to ask, "How am I doing?" Whatever a child's goals and aspirations may be, if all goes well on the developmental journey, he reaches a point at which it is possible to internalize a set of values and judge himself against those values. With a strong sense of personal values, what you might even call a sense of mission, a child, a teenager, or an adult is not so vulnerable to what peers say, what parents say, or what teachers and bosses say. What matters is how they answer that "How am I doing?" question themselves.

Knowing Yourself

We have all encountered people who walk into a room full of true confidence and optimism. They look around as if to say, "What wonderful or interesting thing will I find here?" They seem to light up the room, and other people come alive in their presence. They may not be the most successful people we know, or live in the biggest houses; indeed, they may have chosen to live in small houses and drive old cars so that they can take the time to coach Little League or write poetry or practice law *pro bono.*

Genuine self-esteem is not vulnerable to change from day to day. A child, or an adult, who has it does not crumble when faced with a bad grade, an angry teacher, or a rejecting friend. Those ups and downs are upsetting, of course. But the internal values someone has created, and a sense of how well he or she is progressing toward meeting those values, is not crushed by minor setbacks or even by major tragedies. With self-esteem and self-acceptance, a great kid will weather life's inevitable storms and move forward into wisdom.

ENCOURAGING
SELF-AWARENESS AND SELF-ESTEEM

The first principle of building a child's self esteem may seem counterintuitive: Don't drown him in praise. Children rely on feedback to let them know when they're doing a good job or when they could try harder. Be mindful of all their hard work, but also of times when you could expect more.

Another general principle is that your interest and praise must be honest and heartfelt. If you're distracted by thinking about your day at work when your four-year-old builds an elaborate block castle peopled with his army of action figures, he's not going to feel encouraged when you say, "That's a nice castle" with a flat expression.

If, on the other hand, you excitedly turn to him with a twinkle in your eye and say, "Wow! I'll bet no one could *ever* break into that castle!" you'll be letting your child feel, and eventually internalize, the warm glow of your esteem.

So look and listen carefully to all the uniquely interesting, creative, and funny things that your child says or does. By resonating with his new accomplishments, caring gestures, or imaginative or physical leaps, you will help his self-acceptance and self-awareness grow. When you see and acknowledge through thoughtful feedback that he's risked doing something a tiny bit better or differently than he ever did before, he'll know that he's improving and that his gumption has won your admiration and respect.

The warm attention you give to your child's achievements makes all the difference to him. When he's three months old and flashes you a dazzling smile, or six months old and adeptly picks up a Cheerio with two fingers, or coasts along your sofa and then balances upright for the first time at age one, or builds a block skyscraper when he's eighteen months, or heads a soccer ball for the first time when he's eight, it's your bobbing head and look of delight that makes him feel terrific inside. As a child's repertoire of accomplishments that produce a glow in others increases, his sense of self-worth will, too.

Raising the bar for new tasks is another general principle in growing a child's self-esteem. As I mentioned earlier, one way to support your child's positive "can-do" attitude is to set up any new learning tasks in such a way that he can master each incremental step forward at least 70 or 80 percent of the time. Your child will experience a realistic, self-aware pleasure in his accomplishments when you take pride in his mastery of these small steps.

Eventually, a few well-chosen words will do the trick. When you say, for example, "I'm so glad you were gentle with the gerbil," "That house you drew looks exactly like Aunt Rosie's," or "What a neat way of describing the poem," he's gaining a sense that he does specific things very well indeed. His self-awareness will then start expanding: "I'm someone who takes good care of animals," "I'm learning to draw very well," or "I can really write." As he becomes more prideful of the good things he does, he can also begin to accept some of his weaknesses and transgressions. He will still feel some disappointment or embarrassment about his negative traits; but because he has talents and good qualities, too, he won't be overwhelmed.

For a child to accept all aspects of himself, even his less attractive ones, he will rely on your gentle-but-firm limit setting. The boundaries on his behavior that you impose will make him feel that he can control things he's not proud of. This does not mean thwarting curiosity or mischief. When he's "borrowed" his best friend's new Martian robot and hidden it in his bureau drawer, he'll need you to squat down at his side, look intently into his lowered eyes, and firmly take his two hands in yours while you talk about the seriousness of taking something that doesn't belong to him. You can ask him why he did what he did and talk about how sad his friend must be feeling now without his robot. You'll then suggest an appropriate way to make amends that will counter the deep sense of shame he's experiencing. Over time, your child will come to accept all the good-bad, silly-smart, bashful-bold, jealous-generous aspects of his personality.

Steps to Genuine Self-Esteem

1. Play with your baby and take pride in all the small things he does.
2. Challenge him to get what he wants by gesturing or using words or by encouraging him to take action himself.
3. Keep raising the bar a little on your expectations, always keeping his level of development in mind.
4. Let him see the gleam in your eye when he does something a little more, or a little better, than he did the day before.
5. Respectfully engage with him even when he's not doing "good" things, and then set appropriate limits so that he can gradually acknowledge and come to accept all sides of his personality.
6. As he grows older, help him describe the things he's proud of and the things he's less proud of; this way, his self-awareness and pride become an inner standard that he understands and can articulate.

When the vulnerable teenage years arrive, you child's self-esteem will become exquisitely vulnerable to feedback from his peers: Did he look like an idiot when he sat down uninvited at the lunchroom table where the coolest of the cool kids congregate? When your son has been cruelly teased, you can't take away the hurt; you can, however, balance the hurt with the emotional reassurance of a proud gleam in your eye when he tackles a new skill, or when he delights you with a sophisticated phrase or a perfectly timed punch line.

There will be moments when disappointment strikes deep. If he doesn't make the cut for any of the school teams, don't try to cheer him up by loyally insisting that he was as good as all the other players (unless you honestly think so). Instead, help him refocus on his real strengths: Encourage him to take new lessons in an individual sport he loves so that he can regain pride in his real abilities and his impressive drive to seek a "personal best." If his academic struggles make acceptance at his dreamed-of college look unlikely, make sure he knows he has options: a year off, extension courses in a field he enjoys, resetting his goals so that he can transfer to that college later. Whatever you do, don't "phony up" your reaction. Listen to the disappointment and find opportunities to comment on and resonate with whatever genuine abilities your teen demonstrates. Although self-esteem and self-awareness take time, they will gradually become part of his nature.

7

Internal Discipline
Perseverance and Self-Control

....

Twenty-month-old Nate and his mom were visiting a friend one day. It was a nice spring afternoon, so they sat out in the backyard. The friend had been putting in flowers, and a few empty plastic flowerpots were piled at the edge of the lawn.

Nate had plenty of toys with him, but he marched straight over to the pots, squatted down beside them, and began to fill one with handfuls of soil.

"No, no, Nate," his mom said. "That's dirty! Here, play with your stacking blocks."

Nate was having none of it. He glowered at his mother and pushed the dreary old stacking blocks away. "No!" he said, using one of his favorite new words.

"It's okay," said their hostess. "He's not hurting anything."

Nate's mom sighed inwardly about the dirt that was going to get all over her toddler's cute outfit. But she decided to let Nate take the lead in his project. She sat down beside him and started to fill another pot herself, using the trowel. Again, Nate pushed her away, more emphatically this time. "Me do it!" he exclaimed.

"I guess you want to fill the pot yourself," his mom said, smiling at him and giving him a little squeeze. Then she went and sat down beside her friend.

Nate's gardening project kept him busy and occupied for a precious ten minutes, during which time his mom and her friend were able to have a grown-up conversation and drink a glass of iced tea. Meanwhile, Nate concentrated on filling one of the flowerpots right up to the top and patting the soil down.

When a very dirty little boy proudly dragged his flowerpot over to the adults, his mom was feeling relaxed and calm. She laughed, and brushed Nate off before giving him a hug and telling him he had done a great job of gardening. Nate was flushed with his labors, and with the pride of his accomplishment. Now he was ready to play with his good old stacking blocks again.

What's going on here? Nate's mom had tuned in to her son's signal that he wanted a turn at being in charge of his play. Once she understood, she let him choose a project and gave him space and time to complete it. When this happened, Nate found out that he could signal his mother to let her know that he had his own ideas about how he wanted to spend his time in the sunny garden. His reward was not only to play in the earth and finish a task to his satisfaction but also, more important, his feeling of being "the boss." This took persistence on the part of the little boy. And it took sensitivity from his mom. She could see that interrupting this project would make Nate feel thwarted, even angry. She could see that he had an idea and wanted to see it through to its conclusion. Since he was in no danger, she stayed out of his way.

This seemingly simple little moment in the garden was an important step on Nate's road to becoming a disciplined person, someone with an internal ability to control himself, organize himself, and see a task through to completion. He saw something he wanted to do (fill the flowerpot); he expressed his wish to do that task and not another one (the blocks); he took over the project himself and saw it through to the end. Although his language and conceptual skills are not up to it yet, you can almost hear him saying, "Glad I got Mommy off my back so I could finish this important job."

THE INNER VOICE OF DISCIPLINE

Great kids have drive. They plan; they stick to things; they get things done. How do parents guide kids toward that internal sense of discipline? How do they nurture kids who finish their homework because they have an internal sense of its importance rather than because they want to be rewarded with an iPod if they earn an A on the paper, or because they fear the loss of privileges?

Before we look at how this trait emerges as kids climb the developmental ladder, let's look at what being a disciplined adult involves. Mrs. Jones has self-discipline. She sticks to what she wants to do. She can create a plan and follow it, whether it's at work, where she organizes computer networks for her company, or at home when she is doing her spring housecleaning. She not only follows through on her plan but also commands an effective tool: She has an internal voice that walks her through her plan, saying, "Okay, now you've done A and B. How about C and D? Come on, you can do a little more before lunch and then you'll be able to relax and enjoy your break."

Mrs. Jones's internal voice coaches, comforts, soothes, and encourages her; it is almost as if a mother or father were beside her and providing her with guidance, praise, and support and reminding her of the benefits of her hard work. Her internal "companion" not only helps her stick to her plan but also helps her avoid and resist distraction.

Let's say a colleague at work asks, "How about a coffee break? I need to tell you about what happened yesterday with my kids." Mrs. Jones is in the middle of enacting her plan, so she says, "I want to hear about that, but can you wait a bit? How about coming to lunch with me instead?" She's able to finish what she has planned to finish. She's not easily distracted, even by the temptation of a chat with one of her best friends. At home, when she is helping one of her children with homework or cleaning up after dinner, she is similarly not easily distracted by a telephone call from a good friend, by a desire to put her feet up and relax, or by any other impulse of the moment. She gets things done to her satisfaction and only then turns to the friendly chat or the half-hour on the sofa with a book.

The advantage of this, of course, is that on a day when she doesn't feel well and decides she needs some R&R, Mrs. Jones can relax, put her feet up, and thoroughly enjoy the time off without feeling anxious or guilty or thinking, "I ought to be working." She can plan for hard work and she can plan for fun or relaxation when it's needed. That internal voice tells her that she has earned a few hours or a day off. It is wonderful to have a comforting internal voice that can tell us when we are doing well, keep us on track, and give us a day off here and there.

A World of Distraction

In contrast, take Mr. Smith, whose internal voice is faint at best. Mr. Smith needs to finish a few reports at work, but he is easily distracted by the sound of conversation nearby. He tries to overhear, and turns back to his work only if the voices prove too muffled to understand. Once he gets back to work, he might see other colleagues laughing by the water cooler. He feels compelled to join them and find out about the joke—and his work goes undone. Mr. Smith's internal voice, if it has anything to say at all, will likely castigate him for wasting time and getting to the end of the day with tasks unmet. All evening, he will feel anxious and worried, guilty and uncomfortable. And tomorrow his work still won't be completed.

Now, Mr. Smith is a very bright man. His evaluations often say, "Smith's got enormous potential, great analytical skill, but doesn't seem to work at capacity. His work is uneven, inconsistent, often late, and not of the quality he is capable of." His wife complains in the same way. When he is enjoying himself, playing golf or studying the guitar, he is quite capable of focus and concentration. But when it comes to perseverance through long-winded corporate reports or chores, no inner voice keeps him on the job.

Mr. Smith is not hyperactive or deficient in attention when life is easy. He is an example of an individual who hasn't been able to develop internal discipline—the ability to shape and implement a plan of action and follow it through. When he was younger, various temptations would get him into hot water, and he would be severely disciplined—but that didn't seem to help him change.

When a child is evidencing distractibility, impulsive behavior, and an inability to follow through, we often want to punish that child. We feel that tough, hard, discipline and serious consequences for her actions will help her shape up and become more like Mrs. Jones: a disciplined person who can follow through. But tough love—the punitive, hard-nosed approach—doesn't always work; indeed, punished children often regress and become more impulsive and more distractible, have more difficulty disciplining themselves, and respond only to external sources of discipline. A child may pay attention when a grim adult is right there looking over her shoulder, but as soon as the adult goes out the door, the child's discipline goes out the window.

The kind of discipline we are talking about is not discipline in the sense of punishment. *It is the discipline that helps a child learn to focus and stick to a task until it is finished.* "The goal of discipline is self-discipline" as the pediatrician T. Berry Brazelton says.

Learning to Focus

Meet Lisa. A cuddly, calm baby, she enjoys her mother's warm embrace; she likes to hear her father's gentle voice. She is beginning to focus on the external world and take it in through her senses of sight, hearing, touch, smell, and taste. She waves her hands in front of her face and tries to figure out whom they belong to. She turns her head to the side to see who's looking over the edge of her crib. She's beginning to engage with the world.

As Lisa gains control of her muscles, she begins to organize her movement in conjunction with information gathered from her senses. When her older brother comes loudly into the nursery banging on his toy drum, she startles. When Daddy coos to her as he holds her for a late-night bottle, she calms. When Mommy feeds her and dresses her in a dry, warm sleep suit, she experiences pleasure. Her world seems simple; in fact, it is a full and challenging one. Her senses are at work all the time to connect her with her external world. She is learning to focus, to pay attention.

Why is this earliest ability to focus so important to the development of internal discipline? Because an essential part of discipline is the ability to concentrate on something and follow through. For Lisa, looking at Mommy's face or turning toward the sound of her voice is a goal. She can plan an action, sensing that "Mommy is over there," and turning her head in that direction. This ability to combine an action with information gathered by the senses is the first step toward being focused and planning appropriate action. She is getting her sensory equipment working together as a team.

Emotion: The Fuel of Internal Discipline

Another important step on the developmental ladder involves engagement—that process of falling in love with the world and the important people in it. Engagement means paying attention; it means noticing the sensations we love in the world—warmth, food, laughter—and connecting those pleasures with the people and things around us.

Ten-month-old Timmy discovered one day that if he tweaked Daddy's nose, Daddy would make a funny face, say some words, and then pretend to be a locomotive letting off steam. So Timmy does it again. And again. The game becomes a familiar routine for father and son. Both enjoy it, and they depend on it to reconnect them when they have been separated by Daddy's workday.

Why is engagement so important for internal discipline? Because emotional connection drives actions. Emotions organize a child's senses and actions. In Timmy's game, his perseverance at tweaking his father's nose is orchestrated by the pleasure he takes in the relationship, the joy he feels when his reaching out is answered with funny noises, laughter, cuddles, and smiles.

The relationship draws Timmy to focus on his father and motivates him to be purposeful. For a few weeks, Timmy waits every evening for Daddy to come home so that he can play the whistling-nose game. He plans his action—reaching for Daddy and tweaking—and he gets results. This apparently simple game involves the very beginnings of internal discipline: Tim knows what he wants. He knows what to do to get it. And he is enormously satisfied when his plan works and Daddy pretends to blow off steam.

Disciplined Problem Solving

The next step in achieving organized, internal discipline is a critical one: developing the ability to solve a problem, to create an action plan so that a task can be accomplished. Nate, the toddler you met at the beginning of this chapter, is learning to do this. He has figured out that if he wants something in the kitchen and Daddy is around, he can usually get some kind of treat. (He also knows that this strategy doesn't work as well with Mommy.) One Saturday morning, Nate's mother came downstairs for breakfast and found her husband and son enjoying Oreo cookies and milk.

"The milk is okay. But Oreos for breakfast?"

"He came in the living room where I was reading the paper, grabbed my arm, and practically dragged me over to show me where you keep them!" her husband protested. "He led me right to the cupboard and pointed to the right door so that I would open it and get the cookies out. Of course I did it!" (Daddy is clearly impressed with his son's brilliance.)

Although he can't say more than a few words put together in short phrases, Nate is becoming a master communicator. He knows how to use his gesture language to solve problems and accomplish goals. On that Saturday morning, the goal was an Oreo, and the problem was the high shelf and closed cupboard that kept the cookies out of Nate's reach. By putting two and two together—Daddy and effective gestures—Nate got just what he wanted. His dad's open admiration of his skill was an added bonus!

This kind of problem solving can happen with an eight-year-old who wants Mom to help fix her bicycle and with a twelve-year-old who wants to go to a friend's house and has to figure out whether her mother or father is going to drive. Whatever the problem, solving it is easier when you can enlist someone else, whether an adult or a peer. Shared, multistep problem solving helps children develop the internal discipline of sticking to something until they've worked it out.

If a child successfully takes these three steps—from focus to engagement to problem solving—she is on her way to being a purposeful child who can organize her senses and concentrate her actions on the task at hand. She's on her way to being a disciplined child who will grow into a disciplined adult.

The Internal Voice

Remember Mrs. Jones and her motivating, calming inner voice? How do children move from the early cause-and-effect thinking that Nate displayed to developing an internal voice strong enough so that external structure and challenges aren't necessary to maintain discipline? How does a child become a person who continues to solve problems and take action when no one else is watching? In shared social problem solving, something that continues throughout life, there's someone else to discuss things with, argue with, and help you come to a solution. But what if you're alone, trying to play a game when no one else is in the room?

This is where the imagination comes into play. In the second and third year of life, a child learns to create ideas and symbols.

In typical development, you'll begin to notice that your child is pretending. Her stuffed tiger begins to talk; her dolls begin to misbehave. When this happens, your child is exercising ideas.

During this stage of development, a child begins to describe what she is doing or what she wants: "I want the apple." "Give me the juice." She may even say: "I'm going to get the juice," or "My tiger is going to drink some water." She begins to describe her own actions and project them into the future: "I'm going to hear a story in bed."

During this stage, the voice that will eventually be internal and silent may speak from a child's toys, or she may say things out loud about herself: "I'm a good girl. I put the apple core in the trash." She begins to describe her actions, what she is seeing, or her likes and dislikes: "Mommy, I like the juice, I don't like the banana." She is laying the foundations for her internal voice. A child who can say, "I like the apple," can say to herself, "You're a good girl," or "Put on my boot so I can go outside and play." She can begin telling herself what to do rather than just describing what she wants to do. "Put the apple core in here," she may murmur as she throws away the fruit. "Good girl."

Selma Fraiberg, in her book *The Magic Years*, vividly describes a child's transition from impulses to the use of images and words:

> Gradually, as the mental processes develop, and we can follow this through language development, we find more and more readiness to substitute words and thoughts for action and we increase our expectations for the child, asking him to employ words and thoughts to a larger and still larger extent in dealing with his impulses. But we must remember that months and years go into this education and though we can expect improved control by the end of the third year, this is still a pleasure-loving

little fellow and lapses in control will be frequent and we are not surprised.

To encourage children as they develop this more compli- cated, multilayered way of describing their world and their place in it, we need to help them use symbols, words, and ideas. At first, your daughter may declare, "Give me the juice," which is not much different from simply grabbing the juice. It's an im- pulsive way to express her idea. That's fine, and it's one of the first things we see as children begin to use ideas. But we need to engage them in conversation and help them go one step further: "I want the juice"; and later: "May I have the juice?"

"I want the juice" is different from "Give me the juice" be- cause "I want the juice" expresses a desire. It doesn't have the im- mediacy of "I've got to have it now or I'm going to hit you in the nose." Adding "I want it" means "I have a need; I have a desire." The child is beginning to reflect on her own internal emotion. The *want* is the emotion. She is describing a feeling. Eventually, her emotional ideas will connect in reality to produce an inner running commentary: "I want the juice, but I can't have it until I pick up these toys and put them in the box. Better put them in the box so I can get the juice."

This internal conversation evolves into the internal voice that helps a disciplined child or adult accomplish what she sets out to do. Whether it's preparing a snack or filling out a college applica- tion, the voice is the same: Do this, stick to it, and you'll have a better chance of getting what you want at the end of the task.

Logic and Persistence

Matt is crazy about dinosaurs. He can name them and draw them, and he loves to run around the yard with a few friends pretending they are a fierce herd of *Tyrannosaurus rex*. But as a second grader, Matt has other obligations to fulfill than playing. He has simple family chores to perform, including walking the family's elderly dog slowly around the block and picking up his room. Figuring out how to get what he wants—time to engage in his dinosaur passion—and still meet those obligations calls on Matt's developing skills.

Using his new, still somewhat tentative, internal voice, Matt can say, "If I walk Barney right after school then I can play *T. rex* until supper."

Figuring this out—and explaining it—is an important step for Matt. He is learning what social scientists call "delayed gratification," a critical lesson for all great kids and successful adults. His mother knows the importance of this, and engages him in extended conversations about what he has on his schedule every day and how he will arrange his time so that he can fit it all in. During their conversations, she and Matt can begin to negotiate:

> "Mommy, if I put my pajamas away in my drawer *before* I come down to breakfast, I'll have some time to look at my dinosaur books," he says.
>
> "You're right, Matt. What a great idea. But why do you want to look at the dinosaur books first thing in the morning?"
>
> "Because Mrs. McGuire said that if I can name five dinosaurs without looking at the book I can play with the classroom hamster," he replies.

Mommy is not the only person Matt is learning to negotiate with. His desires power his internal voice to help him work through the things that may not be as much fun but still have to be done.

To increase the logic of that internal voice, nothing beats discussions—the more the better—with your child. As her vocabulary improves, you can question her: "Why do you want this or that?" and "How will you feel if you get it; how will you feel if you don't get it?" Through answering your questions, your child will be able to plan her actions in a logical way. Her internal voice will grow clearer as she practices—and that will build a foundation for the kind of internal voice a disciplined adult uses as a guide through a complex situation to a job well done.

Reflection and Planning

Once a child can listen to and speak aloud her internal voice, she has begun to move to higher levels of reflective thinking. She can weigh the strategies to reach her own goals against one another, seeing which are effective and what to avoid. She can also describe the degrees to which one method holds and another doesn't.

"You don't look too ready to work on that math project," Jenna's mother comments soon after her daughter drags in from the school bus.

"No way, not now! I want to go lie in the hammock because it is so nice outside and it's so dark and gloomy inside. I've been in all day long! It's healthier outside."

To help Jenna form a plan for her afternoon, her mom asks: "If you go out and lounge in the sun now, when are you going to do your homework?"

"Well, I'll go out and lie in the hammock with my magazine for just ten minutes and then I'll come in and work on that project. I promise!" Jenna replies.

Because Jenna can now see the world in gradations, not all-or-nothing, she will be able to stay outside for ten minutes and then remind herself that she has an assignment to do. A child in the all-or-nothing stage thinks she can either play forever or be stuck doing homework forever. As a "gray-area" thinker, Jenna is able to see that she can relax outside for a while and then do her homework for a while. It allows her to plan in a more fine-tuned way—and to enjoy her ten minutes in the hammock. If her break extends into fifteen minutes, her mother may grumble. But with the occasional reminder, Jenna can now make a plan and generally stick to it—which she does.

Self-Evaluation and Discipline

By the age of twelve or thirteen, your child knows important things about herself; she can evaluate her own standards of behavior and her own thoughts and feelings. She can internally pat herself on the back and say, "I did a good job today. I finished that chapter in my book for English, and then I had a great time going out and playing soccer with Jill." She can also recognize poor performance and make an admission: "I did a terrible job at school today. I fooled around and flubbed that French quiz. Now I can't go out with my friends because I have to do more work."

The ability to evaluate yourself and plan accordingly is what consolidates internal discipline. This absolutely critical skill is established in early adolescence and then carries through into the adult years. Realistic self-evaluation connects the internal voice with the demands of the outside world. The internal voice needs to balance between pleasure and pride in jobs well done and disapproval and disappointment in jobs done badly or not at all. By early adolescence, children can scold themselves when they are goofing off and praise themselves when they are doing well. Moreover, they can do this without going overboard: not giving themselves too hard a time when things go badly and not being overly cocky when they do well.

ENCOURAGING
INNER DISCIPLINE

As we have seen, inner discipline is built by encouraging a child's natural drive and interests and by setting loving, respectful limits. When a child's first tiny exploits meet joyful responses, and later when she faces appropriate consequences when she misbehaves, your child will be motivated to work at her goals and will begin to apply the limit setting to herself. All great kids eventually become masters of this far more sophisticated, internalized discipline system.

Although that inner voice sometimes gets shouted down by externals, such as peer pressure, powerful hormonal urges, or the sight of the last chocolate cookie lying unattended on your plate, true self-discipline will eventually arm your child with the fortitude to stay the course—or find her way back to it—and remain focused on her goals.

To develop self-discipline, a child has to learn to act on her own intentions. The very earliest gestural dialogues that parents naturally engage in with babies start building her sense that her actions, driven by her desires, will be greeted by your understanding response. When your five-month-old cries out in an especially piercing way, she's letting you know that her clammy diaper is distressing her. The sight of your caring face peering down at her and the humming sound of your sympathetic murmurs as you pick her up reassure her at the most fundamental level that her world isn't chaotic and that her expressed needs will be met. In a very busy or stressed household, this reassurance is not always a given.

Toddlers who enjoy many playful times with their parents learn to be confident that their actions—prompted by their desires—will usually bring about delightful results. A child learns what it takes to engage you, and by extension the world outside herself, to help her achieve her goals. This happens with lots of practice and the small, achievable steps that bring her closer to reaching her heart's desire.

Let's say your child wants to go out to play. As the two of you walk through the kitchen toward the hall closet to look for jackets and hats, why not comment that your puppy's water bowl "looks empty and we'd better fill it up before we go outside or Daisy will get thirsty!" When your little girl rushes to pick up the bowl, ask whether she'd like to fill it up herself. When she firmly nods her head up and down, proud to be a big girl, ask whether she can reach the faucet. Watch her drag a chair over to the sink. By pretending to have some trouble turning the faucet on, you can find out whether she will take matters into her own hands. Let her carry the filled bowl over to the dog and remind her to put the chair where it belongs so that the two of you can then bundle up and go outside.

By now she is getting impatient to go out. She will race to the closet. Why not look a little befuddled, mumbling, "Where did I put those gloves?" When she finds them and pulls them off the shelf, saying, "Silly Mommy!" perhaps you could run into a few more sartorial snags, such as a "stuck" buckle on your boot. That's a lot of steps she's taken, and problems she's managed to overcome, en route to playing outside in the snow.

What happens next may provide you with an even more valuable teaching tool. Let's suppose your toddler refuses to come inside after the two of you have made a snowman and decorated it with twigs. When she angrily runs away from you and veers towards the busy street next to your house, you'll have to scoop her up and firmly set some limits. It may require a time out, or a nose-to-nose discussion about how she has to use words and not run away when she's angry, or a combination of both, but she's counting on you to help her limit her impulsive behavior.

Your child may appear resentful, but she's emotionally receptive to your calm persistence in setting limits because she experiences you as the source of all her greatest pleasures, joys, and security. In fact, ever since she was a small baby and recognized you as the person who fed her, played with her, and made her feel cozy and secure, your "No, no!" when she pushed her bowl off her high chair tray or yanked her big sister's hair has carried special weight.

During the elementary school years, your child's yearnings and projects will grow more complex and the discipline you give her will become more nuanced. In addition to acknowledging each triumph, and failure overcome, you'll have to be firm and persistent and establish appropriate penalties (time outs, losing television-watching privileges, and forgoing favorite activities, for example). Many long conversations may be needed to help her understand why she's doing what she's doing and why she feels compelled to break the rules sometimes.

As your schoolchild grows older, her ability to stay on task is supported by her internalized sense of discipline. And since staying on task is the sine qua non of accomplishments in academics, the arts, and sports, you'll want to help her take more and more initiative. Don't hover over her as she does her homework, checking to make sure she's aced every answer. Be helpful, be available, but insist that she frame specific questions if she needs help with her work. When she comes to you, armed with questions, she's experiencing herself as a disciplined problem solver ("I've figured out exactly what it is that I don't understand, I haven't melted down, and I've sought information from a tried-and-true source").

When she's nine or ten years old, she'll more frequently turn to outside help in solving her problems: search engines on the Internet, library books, after-school sessions with a teacher, and phone calls to Uncle Tim, who "knows everything." But she'll probably need your help more than ever in anticipating the discipline that will be needed in all the new schoolwork or outside activities. As I mentioned earlier in the book, helping children to "think about tomorrow" helps them identify the feelings they're likely to experience in different situations; it helps them anticipate future hurdles and disappointments and develop game plans to meet them.

If your middle schooler tends to be disorganized, forgets to hand in her homework, or does not study for a test, she's probably anxious about the fallout that she will face. You can explore with her whether a quick call to a friend or an after-school conversation or tutoring session with her teacher might allay some of her fears and help her feel in control of the situation.

One very helpful tactic is to set up a big chalk- or dry-erase board and have your child create her own, outsized calendar. She can draw pictures to jog her memory, or perhaps create a written outline in wacky day-glo colors of her own choosing to note upcoming assignments, team practices, and music lessons. It's fine if you are companionably nearby to supply help if she asks for it, but it's important that your child invest in this external organizer by creating it herself. She can then check off, and own, each of her assignments or activities as she accomplishes them. This kind of visually compelling game plan marks a kind of halfway point on your child's gradual journey from relying on your guiding voice and limits to trusting her own inner voice. The goal is for her to develop an abiding, can-do spirit that empowers her to implement a plan of action and follow it through, step by step.

When parents speak with children and adolescents with warmth and support, but also firmness when needed, they model the internal voice they want their child to have. It helps if they speak to themselves in that same warm, well-regulated way. Disciplined adults speak to themselves in the same voice I hope you use with your child—by turns tender or humorous, demanding or angry, delighted or frustrated, proud or disappointed, firm or indulgent—but always with loving respect.

Steps to Inner Discipline

1. Allow a small child to focus on her interests, whether it is sand castles or finger paints, and applaud her persistence.
2. Engage with the child's interests to increase her pleasure.
3. Participate with the child in solving problems; model and talk about each step toward a solution.
4. Gently but persistently set limits to help the child avoid distraction by the need of the moment. Enlist the child in choosing appropriate penalties and in discussing why setting limits is necessary.
5. Help the child take more and more initiative in organizing her time and choosing her goals. Be available when she needs your support in sticking to her game plan.
6. Ask leading questions that help her figure out what might stand in the way of what she wants; anticipate the hard work and patience that will be needed to achieve her goal.

An inner, disciplined voice will be vital in high school. It will urge a student to go over her Spanish vocabulary words before the end of the week, and remind her to clean out the garage and wash your station wagon if she wants the driving practice for her learner's permit. She may have outgrown the discipline supplied by the outsized calendar and other reminders of her middle school years, and she probably rebuffs, justifiably, your direct involvement in her schoolwork and shows resentment toward any nagging to do her chores, but she still needs help from you in supporting her internalized sense of discipline. Often this may mean testing your rules, trying out the limits.

D. W. Winnicott, in his book *Talking to Parents,* describes this transitional style in an adolescent's life vividly:

> Adolescents quite characteristically make tests of all security measures and of all rules and regulations and disciplines. . . . Why do adolescents especially make such tests? Don't you think it's because they're meeting frighteningly new and strong feelings in themselves, and they wish to know that the external controls are still there? But at the same time they must prove that they can break through these controls and establish themselves as themselves.

Many teenagers may be able to plan ahead, but only in small bursts of concerted effort. You can help your teenager focus on the value of patiently plodding through sequenced, short-term tasks to achieve longer-term goals by listening to her worries and miseries and asking thoughtful questions. As always, help her tease out her interests and passions and follow her conversational lead.

If, for example, your daughter announces that she wants to go to college because she can't wait to get away from home, or that she's dying to have her own car and live off campus, or that she wants to study acting instead of being a Fulbright scholar, empathize with her passion. That's what will motivate her to think seriously about the challenges she's choosing and to evaluate whether her plans will achieve her heart's desire. She'll be more willing to show resolve and behave in a disciplined way if she feels her goals are respected. Once they leave home, adolescents need to take care of themselves not just in the basics but also through fine-tuned, healthy judgments. A disciplined young adult goes to college able to balance new experiences, new academic demands, and, often, new temptations. A disciplined adult enters relationships ready to negotiate and to compromise; he is able to defer his own desires, at least temporarily, to the needs of a partner or a child.

Although a young person's goals will usually shift over and over again during the next few years, her growing ability to attend to her inner voice of discipline will enable her to defer instant gratification much of the time and to keep her eye on the future—as all great kids do.

8

Creativity and Vision
A Rich Internal Life

....

In a preschool classroom, two little girls and a little boy are play-ing a game with their teacher. She's sitting on a round stool in the middle of the room, and the children are circling her, say-ing, "What shall we play?"

"It's your turn to decide," the teacher says.

"I know, let's do your hair," says one little girl, who re-cently had her long hair cut short.

The little boy says, "At the barber they put a sheet over me when I got my hair cut," and he runs to get a canvas tarp from the painting area. It's a little splotched with finger paint, but it will do fine.

The children drape the teacher, and they're ready to style her hair. But then they run into a problem: They don't have any combs or brushes, and the teacher says she doesn't want them to use scissors.

"This is a pretend haircut," she reminds them, "so no scissors."

One of the girls looks around the classroom. When she spies the plastic cooking tools arrayed in the toy kitchen, she runs over and picks up a bright red fork and a yellow spoon.

"These can be the brush and comb," she says, delighted with her innovative idea.

The kids surround their teacher, mussing her hair and spinning it around the plastic implements.

"I *know*," the little boy shouts joyfully. "This is the barbershop café!"

This true story, which I witnessed recently when visiting a classroom, shows preschool kids in their element. As they play with their beloved teacher, they invent a scene that helps the children to relive their real-world experiences (the recent haircuts) and allows all three youngsters to act like grown-ups with real jobs. Their game also calls on their resourcefulness: In the absence of real hairstyling tools, they look around at the environment and find something else to use. Then one of them reinvents the situation, watching the fork and spoon at work on the teacher's hair: "Yup," says he, "we're a barbershop *and* a café," pleased with his invention.

Children call on their imaginations all the time, whether they are telling a story, making up and acting in a play, building castles, or creating internal visions when a teacher reads to them from a book.

SEEDS OF CREATIVITY

Children move comfortably in the world of imagination all the time. Play is their work, a critical developmental task. They are sustained in this by internal images of their parents and other important figures in their lives who give them a secure base from which to learn and experiment: "I know Mommy loves me and is proud of me that I'm being a good boy [or girl] in school, even though I can't see her," they might be thinking.

A World of Delight

From the beginning, a newborn baby takes in sights and sounds. In the first stage of development—self-regulation and interest in the world—babies look and listen and learn to calm down. They take an interest in what's going on and figure out ways to respond. Parents pay attention to these responses, noticing, for example, that their baby likes to turn toward a high-pitched voice, but not a low-pitched one. Sammy has a two-year-old sister who has a high, squeaky voice. Whenever he hears her, he immediately turns his head and looks her way. His mother notices and tries to imitate Jean's high-pitched voice—and Sammy looks a little more. Sammy will turn to Daddy's lower, more rumbly voice, too, but not as readily.

Sammy's parents take advantage of his natural inclination to help him explore new territory. Their son likes to look at a bright red triangle that revolves on the mobile hanging over his bed, so his mother puts on a red hat while standing off to Sammy's left a little bit. And Sammy does indeed turn his eyes to take in the hat.

The important thing here is that Sammy's parents are responding to their son's natural inclinations—things that he may have been born with or may have inherited. Or—who knows?—Sammy may be showing an interest that developed through chance occurrences in the first moments and days of his life.

It doesn't much matter how or why the baby's interest occurred. But when his parents tune in to him, Sammy feels at some deep level, long before he can even express it in words or any other way, that his individual, unique capacities are being acknowledged. He's not being treated like a machine; he's being responded to as a special little individual. This helps him to calm himself, to focus, and to take a wider interest in the world.

By noticing what babies find fascinating in their surroundings, parents help their infants experience the world in a pleasurable, joyful way. They are tuning into their emotions. Excitement, joy, and curiosity become attached to the motor pattern of looking. Looking is delightful. Parents start a dialogue with their baby, expanding into other sights, sounds, sensations, and rhythmic activities. They follow the baby's lead and make sounds together, move together, look together, explore interesting toys together. In the microscopic moments of every day, every minute, every second, parents foster their baby's natural interests by tuning into individual characteristics and building his pleasure in a loving relationship.

For these interactions to happen and build upon themselves, some degree of structure is necessary. A calm, well-fed baby is a baby who can afford to explore and be curious. Between regular sleep/wake cycles and eating cycles, a baby's preferences become clear. These early games are at the root of a child's imaginative engagement with his world.

Creativity and Desire

As babies develop, they learn to link pleasure with more complicated behavior such as swaying to music, trying out words, playing with colors. They begin linking their emotions not only with more complicated motor patterns and gestures but also with symbols and words. This is important for creativity because creativity is thinking *from* your emotions. It is thinking from your inner desires, being inspired from within.

Albert Einstein talked about creativity when he said that as a preschooler he was taking imaginative trips—but not just to the playground, the schoolyard, or some make-believe Never-Never Land. He also somehow held onto his "childish" sense of wonder and awe:

> I sometimes ask myself how did it come that I was the one to develop the theory of relativity. The reason, I think, is that a normal adult never stops to think about problems of space and time. These are things which he has thought about as a child. But my intellectual development was retarded, as a result of which I began to wonder about space and time only when I had already grown up.

When we simply respond to the external world in predictable ways, we are not being creative. We may be organized; we may be orderly; we may be efficient, but no one would call us creative. But when the lightbulb goes on inside and we experience a flash of insight, the inspiration for a new story, a new tune, a new experiment, a new business venture—that's creativity, that's vision. In this way, our emotions express themselves in innovative ideas and designs.

A child who can take the initiative and follow his own desires has a head start on creativity. Parents can encourage this by letting him make choices and follow his natural interests. Perhaps he likes the necklace around your neck and he reaches for it. Let him take it off and inspect it; maybe he will taste it or hold it in the light. Watch his joy. Offer him an even shinier necklace. Look to him to make the next move. He may throw his necklace on the floor to see what happens when the necklace lands and bounces, making, for him, a satisfying noise.

If you allow your child to set the agenda and decide what to do next when he is taking the initiative, you are giving him the sense that his ideas and his agendas are important. You are letting him be the kind of person who comes up with a new idea rather than just reacting and responding.

There is a big difference between structuring activities for your child and challenging the child to follow his own inclinations. All you have to do is relax a little bit, be patient, and watch what your child is doing. Don't try to come up with a bag of tricks. Watch what your little guy is doing, take his lead, and then build on it. Once you do that, you will discover the rhythm of creating spontaneous, flowing interactions. Responding to the often-surprising reactions of a small child challenges him to have more ideas and enjoy trying new things. Directing his activities or thwarting them to avoid a mess will only dampen his excitement and imagination.

When toddlers begin to use words and ideas in pretend play, it is just as important to let them take the lead, as that good preschool teacher did in the story that opened this chapter. Instead of being the stage manager, let your child take the lead; you can be sure that something more interesting will happen when you do so.

Letting a child speak for himself allows for the creative use of language and the natural use of words. If you reward your nineteen-month-old with candy for saying, every time he sees a new person, "Hello, Mr. So-and-so" or "Hello, Mrs. So-and-so," you are training him by rote. But if your child has lots of experience greeting delightful individuals—Mommy, Daddy, his brother or sister, or a favorite friend or teacher—and has enjoyed the playful experiences that result from such greetings, he will learn to say hello on his own. It might begin with a flirtatious glance or wave, a gleam in his eye, and a welcoming sound before he buries his head in Mommy's shoulder or hides behind her legs. Eventually, he'll get to "hi" or "hello," or even rush to his grandfather with an idea for a funny game. Unlike a rote response, his greeting will come from the inside. It will be a salutation that is formed through natural, spontaneous interactions with you and others; as he grows, it will become part of his style of engaging with other people.

Similarly, if you show your child how to dress dolls or suggest where the toy car should go, his play will be pretty dull and structured. If your little boy tells you to be the policeman blocking his car, you can say, "Stop, thief!" Your son will grin mischievously and go around the policeman right into the house. If your child throws the car or kicks the car, instead of scolding him you can talk for the car and say, "Ouch! That hurts! What are you doing?" He may kick the car again. You can say, "Help! I need a doctor, I need a doctor," and so on. As your child learns more subtle ways of communicating, the possibilities of imaginative play will be unlimited.

Imagination and Logic

When your child begins to use ideas logically, becoming involved in asking and answering the big "W" questions—where, what, who, and why—not only his logic but also his imagination will grow.

Say your three-year-old pulls all the cushions off the couch:

"What are you doing?"
"I'm making a castle."
"Who will live there?"
"Just me, not Susie."
"Why?"

And so on. You can see that just telling a child not to mess up the couch will not lead in such a lively direction.

All kinds of situations, from dialogues about games, meals, trips, even bedtime, encourage both logic and fantasy. Dialogues with children who are asking the "W" questions encourage them to express their wishes, think about connections, and come up with new ideas. When these new ideas are not nipped in the bud, a child's mind and imagination expand and his confidence in his own ability to communicate ideas grows.

As your child's perceptions and conversations express even greater nuances and matters of degree, you can encourage him to be the one generating the ideas. Rather than asking a new reader what happened in the story he has just finished, you can ask: "What did you like best about the story?" By listening to your child's answers you can find out what he thinks is funny, whether he looked more closely at the words or the pictures, and what imaginative responses he has had to the book. You're looking for your child's opinions, ideas, and feelings—not right or wrong answers.

Creativity in the Classroom

The freedom to explore new ideas without worrying about a "right" answer is not often encouraged in schools. In *The Nature of the Child,* Jerome Kagan shows how important this is to creativity:

> While most intelligent children are not necessarily creative, most creative children are intelligent. But their creativity is based on three other characteristics: They have a mental set to search for the unusual; they take delight in generating novel ideas; and they are not unduly apprehensive about making mistakes. A major

hallmark of the creative person is some indifference to the humiliation that can follow a mistake. This attitude gives the child freedom to attempt mental experiments that may fail and to consider high-risk solutions without worrying too much about their potential failure.

Very early, whether at school or at home, we tend to teach "to the test"; we put too much emphasis on getting the right answer and not enough on conceptual thinking and reasoning. Unfortunately, current national education efforts are focusing too much on learning set material at the expense of innovative thinking and creativity. To meet testing standards, many schools are encouraging rote teaching methods. In our national education efforts, we need to revise the way we test and evaluate so that we can foster, and treasure, creativity and innovative thinking.

A young teacher I know spent a great deal of time during the autumn semester putting on a Halloween play with her fifth-grade class. The teacher was new in the school, and she wanted to impress the parents and her colleagues with how well her students could do in the Halloween assembly. So she gave up class time in language arts and history to help her students plan the play. The students wrote their own play based on a story from the Salem witch trials; they voluntarily stayed in from recess to sew costumes they had designed. One student, who could play the guitar, figured out how to make eerie sound effects. Instead of memorizing a set script, the students were able to express their own ideas and identify and practice their own talents. One said: "I'd like to have the a part in the play, but I'm better at painting than at talking out loud on stage. I'm going to paint sets." This is the kind of comparative, gray-area thinking that children begin to do well as they move into a more reflective stage.

The class writers took joy in inventing dialogue for the characters; a boy who was very shy was able to show off his musical ability when he invented a whole percussion score; a student who loved history had done extra research to capture the details of the colonial costumes. Moreover, the children found ways to cooperate with each other, finding creative solutions to challenges such as how to assign a role for each person in the class, how to bolster the timid kids, and how to rein in the more aggressive ones for the sake of a shared project's success.

These things happened because the students had reached a stage in their development at which they could think in more complex ways and were getting better at seeing and negotiating social hierarchies. But these things also happened especially because the teacher responded to the children's ideas and initiatives instead of passing out a photocopied script and getting them to learn their parts by rote, use recorded music, and rent their costumes.

Although there were a few rough moments, the performance went off well and received an enthusiastic ovation. Afterwards, the principal asked the teacher to come see him in his office in the morning. She spent a sleepless night worrying that she was to be reprimanded for using class time to work on a play instead of strictly following the rules of her daily lesson plans.

Luckily, this teacher's principal recognized innovation when he saw it. "I just wanted to let you know that I thought your kids showed great creativity in that play," he said. "Not only did they learn their history, they brought it alive for all of us."

Creativity and Self-Awareness

Toward adolescence, children learn to evaluate their own thoughts, to say, for example, "I'm really disappointed about that paper. Last time I didn't care as much" or, "I think that boy should be suspended, but maybe only a few days because he didn't mean to hurt anyone." Evaluating themselves and comparing themselves and their thoughts to their own internal standards or to values held by parents, teachers, and peers are developments that require new levels of reflective thinking.

This kind of comparative thinking helps a child evaluate his ideas and creative endeavors. "This is a really good poem, this is a new way of saying something," he might think; or, "Yes, I just wrote this, but it sounds like a Hallmark card and it's kind of lame." The difference between a promising student poet and a corny, sentimental one can rest in how well he can evaluate his own work.

Artists, inventors, and writers need to be both creative and analytical. My colleagues and I did an interesting study that sheds light on this. We evaluated two groups of children—those with severe learning disabilities and those who had none—and we asked them questions that we thought would interest them. We found that the children with severe learning problems and special needs tended to be more structured and rote in their responses, but the other group tended to be more creative and reflective. When the children were asked what they thought of bosses, those with special needs were inclined to say that "parents are bosses, teachers are bosses, policemen are bosses," and so forth, reciting a rote list. Children without special needs tended to give answers such as: "I don't like being bossed, but sometimes I guess I need to be bossed if I'm being mean to my brother or sister and therefore it's okay. So there are good bosses and bad bosses depending on how well they know when I need to be bossed."

It would have been easy to conclude that children with special needs have processing problems and are therefore capable only of a more rote, structured type of learning. But that would have been a mistake. When we asked ourselves what the children without the processing problems were doing, we realized that their responses involved two steps of thinking. They were including their personal experiences with bosses and generating fresh ideas from those perspectives. They then put that in a reflective and analytical context by pointing out different categories of bosses.

When asked the same question, older children and graduate students drew analogies from Shakespeare and other literature and described more types of bosses and more categories of autocratic behavior. But they followed the same basic process in which their personal, emotional experiences generated the ideas and made the lightbulbs go on; then they moved by way of a reflective and analytical process to put those feelings into a logical framework.

All our thinking requires both the generative and the analytical. If we just use the analytical without the generative, we tend to make rote lists. Such a response represents a very low level of reflection. Conversely, if we use only the generative imaginative kind of thinking, we may get interesting nonsense. On the other hand, if we use both the generative part and the reflective part, we tend to produce a creative response. When a child is writing an essay or analyzing a book, or comparing two historical interests, he needs to do both.

After our analysis, we went back and started working with the special needs group in a different way. We began to work from their emotions, from their personal experiences. We developed emotionally based teaching. We did the things that I have just described to you at each stage of development: fostering the child's unique individual processing patterns, focusing on each child's initiative, getting that lightbulb to go on.

Then, as we were playing catch-up with these special needs children, we started with the basics—the kinds of skills a younger child might be working on. We worked on these basics, however, with an eye to the interests of the children. For example, we might play a game of throwing and catching a ball with the goal of eliciting joy and pleasure and relatedness. We tried to work through all the stages of development. What we found was that children with special needs, like their peers without special needs, could become creative and innovative and reflective about the things that interested them. Within their levels of intellectual development, *all* children appear to be capable of innovative, creative thinking and action.

Creativity Through the Life Cycle

Creativity is a quality that enriches us throughout life. Innovation and creativity are needed in adolescence, in adulthood, in marriage and other close relationships, in parenthood, and in the challenges of getting along in the workplace.

We all have met people who spout the opinions, often using the exact words, of the last person they spoke to or the last radio talk-show host they listened to. We recognize that these adults can't "think for themselves," nor can they express their ideas in their own unique ways. They don't seem to be able to think things through and come up with their own ideas and their own language to express them; instead, they parrot platitudes. In the absence of vision and imagination, the challenges of adulthood can force people into narrow opinions and rigid positions.

Adults who have had their creativity encouraged during their developmental stages find it easier to develop the new levels of reflective thinking and empathy that are necessary to get along with a spouse and to raise children. All kinds of imagination, sensitivity, and creative enterprise are needed to make a home in a new city, to balance family and work, to comfort a spouse when he or she loses a parent, to help a child who is struggling in school, or to help an aging mother come to terms with giving up aspects of her independence. Every day brings challenges that require adults to adapt anew while maintaining a strong sense of separateness, uniqueness, and value. This takes vision. When the future is no longer infinite, a new kind of imagination is needed. The broad stage that we imagined we would shine on when we were in college turns out to be smaller than expected. We may not have built skyscrapers, made huge fortunes, become ambassador to Paris, or won the Pulitzer Prize. But mature vision helps us see the greatness of smaller-scale achievements: a child we have stayed close to in spite of a divorce; a neighborhood garden we have nurtured and supported; a job that has sustained us and contributed usefully to our community. Creativity is not the same as worldly success or celebrity.

ENCOURAGING
CREATIVITY AND VISION

Creative people seem to have a visionary sense of the possibilities that lie just beneath the surface—or beyond the horizons—of their day-to-day lives. You can stir up this ability in your child as he grows from infancy to young adulthood by encouraging his natural interests; these propel his curiosity and exploration of the world.

Creativity begins budding in the first year of life, when your baby begins to sense that what comes from him is worthwhile. He knows this because he can count on you, or other loving caretakers in his life, to respond to his looks, gestures, and movements, even though he doesn't yet use words. As you follow his lead as he crawls around the floor, he'll be more than simply tickled by your antics; he'll know the joy of experiencing himself as a leader, as an initiator. If you put a big, fluffy pillow in front of him, see whether he'll crawl over, under, or around it. If you copy his behavior, he'll get a sense of his own importance. By letting him take spontaneous fun in an unexpected direction, he'll come to know that it's rewarding to venture off the beaten track.

By enthusiastically responding to all of your child's first steps towards creativity, you encourage him to be a trendsetter and not merely a follower. When he's using words to express ideas between the ages of three and five, pretend play can explore newer, richer plots. If he keeps reenacting similar dramas in which beautiful princesses are scared by sharp-toothed wolves—and you've assumed the big, bad wolf's role ten times—try throwing him a curve ball. Have your wolf fall down, bump his elbow, and cry for his mommy. Mixing in unexpected actions helps your child "think outside the box."

When he's in grade school and writing a story about an imaginary trip to the twenty-second century, show a keen interest in his ideas. Remind him of how he felt in the planetarium. Ask him about the sights and sounds his character will be experiencing; see whether your questions can spark a more complex story line.

As he climbs the developmental ladder, help your child use a variety of senses and skills. If he's especially adept at drawing, suggest he make up a story about the picture he's created. If he shies away from art projects, but is a real chatterbox, see whether he would like to try his hand at sketching a scene that he's just described to you.

Even musical chairs can be a chance for innovation. Perhaps each time the music stops, the children could assume different positions, sometimes sitting with their legs folded, Indian-style; at other times they might balance themselves on the edge of their seats, hands in the air and feet off the floor. Encourage your child to use his body and his senses creatively, both by himself and with others.

When your child is in middle school and turns his attention to sports, or solitary pursuits such as music and art, you can help sustain these interests by encouraging him first to pay adequate attention to mastering some fundamental skills. All too often children see the finesse of a professional dancer or a perfect drawing; but when they don't see evidence of that kind of giftedness or flair in their own style, they give up too soon.

Although there's no substitute for mastering the basic strokes of a game, or for playing musical scales, or for lots of sketching, it's important for you and your child to explore less rote or rigid ways of making these skill-building tasks more enjoyable. Perfecting scales, repeating a shot just as one particular coach prescribes it, or copying a drawing exactly are exercises that go better when there is some variation.

If your child is encouraged to master the basics by putting his own unique spin on the process—and is reassured that there's no rule book decreeing that only one method will breed success—the joy of creativity and adaptability will keep his interest from flagging. Reassure him that his own ideas shouldn't be put on hold until he "knows everything there is to know."

In her book *Mindfulness,* Ellen Langer, a professor of psychology at Harvard, emphasizes that if we are to allow intuition and creativity, we need to escape mind-sets and rigid rules: "When our minds are set on one thing, or on one way of doing things, mindlessly determined in the past, we blot out our intuition and miss much of the present world around us. If Archimedes had had his mind set only on taking a bath, he probably would not have discovered the displacement of water."

When your child is around eleven or twelve years old, he'll be demonstrating a more advanced capability for reflection, what we call anticipatory or probabilistic thinking. Encourage him to speculate with you by asking questions: "Well, what might happen if . . . "; "If I do this, I'll get this result, but if I do that, what could be the consequences?" Conversations during the late teen years will continue to focus on the future. Challenge your child to articulate how he sees the world now and how he'd like to see it in the years ahead, particularly in those areas in which he has demonstrated a creative interest. Respect his own ideas, even those that might seem trivial at first hearing. Seemingly silly ideas may well lead him through association to come up with better ones. Great ideas come in unexpected ways.

Encouraging Imagination and Innovation

1. Value and respond to your baby's natural interests.
2. Ask questions that lead his ideas in new directions.
3. Encourage him to use all his senses and parts of his body in a variety of ways.
4. Spur a child to master the fundamentals of a particular field or activity in his own unique way.
5. Encourage exploration and inquiry; avoid jumping on mistakes.
6. Avoid rote learning. Engage a child's personal experience and interests in reading, writing, and all forms of study.
7. Encourage a child to think about and express his fantasies and vision for the future in all kinds of writing, painting, and music.

There is a developmental pathway to creative thinking, and we need to pay attention to it both for children and for ourselves. An innovative thinker keeps asking himself questions: "What do I really feel about this?" "What do I believe about this?" "What are my deep personal opinions?" Start with those reflections and then evaluate your personal opinions against logic and against other people's opinions. But keep your personal opinions or your feelings and desires in mind.

A colleague of mine took a class designed to help fiction writers break through their blocks and put words down on paper. In the first class, the teacher handed around black-and-white photographs and asked the class to write for fifteen minutes about what they saw. "Don't cross out, don't go back, don't edit yourself," she said. "There are no right or wrong answers here. Just look at the picture and see where it takes you."

In the silence of the class, pencils flew across the paper. When the timer ran down, the writers were amazed not only that they had written so many words but also that fifteen minutes had flown by. Most of them had managed to go deep inside themselves to discover their reactions to the images in the prints.

"You turned off your internal editor and just got your own reactions and feelings down, without censoring or questioning them," the teacher said. "Now, turn that editor back on and revise those paragraphs before our next meeting. I think you'll find that there is a lot of value in those first pages."

This teacher did with those self-conscious, blocked adults what you can do with your kids or for yourself to foster creativity. Begin where you are and follow those impressions, feelings, and ideas. Great things can come of it.

Creativity goes to the heart of the goals that we as parents have for our great kids. Creativity and vision allow human beings to think innovatively, to imagine the future, to "roll with the punches" of everyday life and come up with workable solutions. More than that, they allow us to find new ways to make our environments healthier and our classrooms, offices, boardrooms, and family homes more welcoming, compassionate, innovative, and nurturing places for everyone.

Creativity is a quality that we recognize, celebrate, and value—and it has to do with much more than the arts. Not everyone can be a Thomas Edison, a Benjamin Franklin, or a Marie Curie; nor can everyone discover a cure for a disease. But most of us have the ability to be more innovative and have more vision than we do now. It has a lot to do with the way we look at the world, the way we ask ourselves questions, the ways we try out new ideas. As adults, some of us may feel it's too late, that the die is cast. But creativity can be reawakened in adults—and one of the best ways to do that is to connect with our children and marvel at the creativity within them.

9

Logical Thinking
Making Sense of the World

· · · · · · · · · · · · · · · · · · · ·

The summer before Charlie began second grade, he started worrying about being shorter than his sister Laura, who's just about
a year younger than he is. He worried about it a lot. He was
self-conscious when they went to the pool and when they
played in the backyard. He cringed with embarrassment when
visitors asked Laura, "And is this your little brother?"

Charlie chewed on this problem as he lay in bed at night. He
tried to imagine a time when he would be taller than Laura, which
his mom said might happen one day. But it hadn't happened yet!

Then, one morning, he said to his mom, "It's not so bad to
be smaller than Laura."

His mother was surprised to hear this, because she'd been
aware of his feelings.

"Why not?" she asked him.
"Well, you're older than Daddy, right?"
"Yes, I'm a year older than Daddy," she agreed.

"And Daddy is a whole lot bigger than you. But you're just as funny as Daddy is, and just as nice. And you're a lot smarter than he is at computers."

Satisfied with this solution, Charlie ran out to play.

Charlie's thought process, based in the reality of his family, was a complex operation suffused with emotion. He had to work through a large set of facts, think about his own feelings, make comparisons, and test his conclusions by discussing them with his mother. He's not finished yet, but Charlie is well on the way to using reality-based thinking and logic to engage the world and make sense of what he finds there.

Rational thought is the ability to make sense of the world. We collect information and use this ever-expanding body of knowledge to create connections among facts, causes, and results. We use this skill in school and college, at our jobs, and in our relationships, from the most casual to the most intimate, but there can be wide variations in how well we do this.

Achieving reality-based, logical thinking is a goal we want for our children, not just to survive but to understand the world in the most expansive way possible. We would hope our children will be logical in all areas of living—their social lives, their appreciation of history and science, their ability to solve computer problems, their ability to read the subtle cues in the most intimate relationships. And we can help them get there.

We all know adults who are highly logical in their professions, say in the world of computers, but are illogical, indeed "clueless," in other parts of life, such as dating or politics or competition at work. Logic doesn't always operate at the same level across the board. A person can be logical in one sphere and not in another.

Take Mr. Franklin, a computer engineer, who is socially awkward. People can't tell whether he is a clown or a klutz, and they respond by teasing him. He doesn't understand their responses and loses his temper. At the same time, he is an extraordinarily gifted programmer, much valued for his skills. Fortunately, his boss takes his momentary upsets and seemingly "illogical" behavior as part of his brilliance.

A different person may not be a technological whiz but applies logic well to social situations. Take Ms. Sullivan, an excellent manager: She understands people and can organize her staff in a way that makes up for differing personalities. She can also evaluate her own biases, her tendency to side with particular viewpoints, and correct for them in her written discussions. She knows when she has enough information to draw conclusions, but she also knows when she needs to consult others. Although she is not brilliant in the accepted sense, she has what people call "emotional intelligence." She can apply reasoning skills to her spouse, her children, and her friends. She can read their subtle signals. She can read between the lines. And she can do it all quickly, even when she's under stress, tired, or overloaded with work. She rarely falls into the trap of becoming an all-or-nothing thinker. She thinks in relative degrees, whether she is assessing people or considering probable business outcomes.

THE STAGES OF LOGIC

To engage in reality-based thinking, children must first be engaged in the world outside themselves and get to know it. To gather this information, they rely on their senses—seeing, hearing, tasting, touching, and smelling the world around them.

Discovering the World Outside

Like the other traits that combine to create a great kid, progress toward logical thinking begins with the first stage in development when babies are beginning to take in the world of sights and sounds outside themselves, yet they still remain calm and well regulated. An infant's first task in logical thinking is to take in the external world and to see a full picture of what surrounds him. This process begins in the first months of life as the baby looks and listens, smells and tastes, and moves his body to snuggle against his mother or simply for the joy of wiggling around.

Most of us know the story about the elephant and the blind men: Each blind man described a different animal based on the part he was touching—flanks, tail, trunk, and ears. This fable shows that if we consider only one aspect of something, we'll see, feel, touch, hear, and emotionally resonate with only one small part of a more complex picture. We become familiar with the tail, but take it for the whole beast. Just as you can't understand the totality of an elephant by acquainting yourself with only its tail, you can't realistically identify what it is that you are trying to understand without assessing it by using all your senses of sight, sound, touch, and smell. That's what babies do every waking moment.

Logical thinking also means being able to embrace the world with a sense of trust and pleasure. Without this ability, a baby can look, listen, smell, and taste the world, but not use the information she gathers because she doesn't trust it. If positive, loving, and warm interactions with her caregivers are absent, she may become suspicious and scared; she may even withdraw and avoid engagement. To learn, children need to be willing to trust not only what they see but also the relationships they have with others who can provide information. To launch that learning process, we need to work to make the external world and the world of relationships pleasurable for the infant.

Purposeful Actions and Recognizing Patterns

On the next leg of the journey toward logical thinking, a child develops the ability to interact with the world purposefully; for example, a baby reaches for a rattle and examines it or an older child grabs a pencil, preparing to write, when the teacher is giving instructions. It is as simple as needing to touch the floor to see whether it's hard, or squeezing a balloon to see whether it's soft. Being able to act on the world is a critical step toward understanding that world. You can't figure things out unless you explore them. This passion to understand how the world works is the beginning of scientific reasoning.

Moreover, as babies quickly discover, action usually leads to reaction. A baby smiles, and Mommy smiles back. A baby coos, and Daddy laughs and coos back. Touching Daddy's nose leads to a certain feeling in the fingers and maybe a sound from Daddy. Squeezing a rattle creates a noise. Every action that is purposeful can lead to a reaction—and that is the beginning of cause-and-effect thinking, even before ideas become part of a baby's consciousness.

This is thinking at its most basic level. The exchange of smile for smile, frown for frown, gives your baby his first experience with cause-and-effect reasoning. Acting with sounds, expressions, and motion is the beginning of logic—and it begins as early as the second half of the first year of life.

The next step in logic is being able to combine actions into a pattern, such as searching for a favorite toy and grabbing parents by the hand to show them what you want and get them to help you. This skill is also involved as a toddler figures out how a jungle gym on the playground works—"Oh, I have to climb over this thing and around this thing and up these steps to get to the slide. Wheee! Okay, now I have to do it again." This requires recognizing patterns and taking a sequence of steps to reach a goal. Going down a slide, finding the toy, coaxing parents to give a big hug, or stacking blocks into a tower requires action steps, arranged in a pattern.

Pattern recognition is essential for critical thinking. By engaging with your child in multiple steps to solve problems together, you are helping build higher-level thinking skills.

Logic and Ideas

The next step toward logic adds a new dimension: the ability to use ideas. Children usually develop this ability between eighteen and twenty-four months. At this stage, a child can translate actions—searching for a hidden object, building a tower, climbing an obstacle course—into ideas. At this stage, a child can begin to experiment not only in the concrete world of toys and playgrounds but also in her mind. She doesn't have to search all over the house for a cookie; she can picture where that cookie might be. She can picture the cookie jar, the pantry cupboard, or the hidden drawer where Mommy tends to put things that she doesn't want her daughter to find. She can search in places that she has thought about *in advance* by using ideas.

Through the power of ideas, children also begin to use pretend play to think. They can put a doll or a stuffed bear through an obstacle course. They can also combine ideas in new ways to develop new thoughts. Symbolic thinking—images and words—enables them to picture their world and play with it inside their heads.

Logic and the "W" Questions

If learning to use ideas goes well, children reach the stage where they actually combine ideas together. When you ask, "*Why* is it dark out?" your child can say, "Because the sun isn't shining." Or "*Why* is it cold?" "Because the wind is blowing." A child can now combine ideas together logically and take part in elaborate dialogues and discussions. She's able to understand her world in a new way. This is what we mean when we say a child has reached the age of rational, logical thinking—usually between the ages of three and four years. When you or the child asks the "W" questions (who, what, when, and where), she is learning to combine ideas with logical bridges.

Around this time, a child begins to appreciate the difference between fantasy and external reality. This is a significant emotional accomplishment. Establishing a sense of reality means that we have to invest the world outside ourselves with some of our own emotions—with some value, some interest, some trust. Being able to tell whether an apple or a monster is a figment of our imagination—something we have invented—is a big step. In our dreams, which are all imagination, that apple tastes mighty good, and the monster is really scary.

A little girl I know made up a story about going to Disney World even though she didn't really go there. "Why did you do that?" I asked her. She said, "Because it felt so good. It felt almost as good as when I really go there." At times, make-believe can be almost as good as reality for some children. That's why they may elect to spend a lot of time in make-believe worlds.

Children escape into fantasy all the time. This can be wonderful. There are several critical steps a child needs to take in order to learn to recognize the boundary between fantasy and reality. First, children have to form relationships with others in the outside world, usually their caregivers. Starting in infancy, these others represent external reality. When your eight-month-old pulls your hair and you squawk, the sound is coming from outside the child. She gets a sense of the difference between what's inside her and what's outside her. When, a little later on, she involves you in building a fort, as opposed to just playing on her own, she receives further confirmation of the world outside herself. She sees that her parents are not just toys but people who can do things that she can't do. She sees that you exist outside her.

Later on, when your child engages in pretend play, you can sometimes join her. When her stuffed piggy goes "oink, oink," you can ask what the piggy wants to eat. By joining in with your child's game, you've introduced an external voice, another imagination besides her own. Sharing pretend play brings two imaginations together, which also establishes a difference between what is "inside me" and what is "outside me." When you ask a child, "Why do you want to go to the park?" it's the voice of reality coming from the outside. You are a live human being who is asking her a question and judging her answer: "Well, I know it's fun there, but you have to wait until I finish cleaning up. Then I'll come with you."

Negotiations and opinion-oriented discussions help establish a boundary between a child and the reality of the outside world. These negotiations can be highly charged. Your child's desires may reflect her dependency, independency, aggression, loving feelings, frustration, or excitement. Meanwhile, she must gradually learn that her feelings may not be the same as what is actually outside her.

If parents are too punitive, too permissive, or too detached and can't engage with the child's demands in a regulated, harmonious way, it can make it harder for a child to establish the boundary between what is imaginary and what is real. She may prefer to escape into fantasy. A calm response to each of her feelings in the course of the normal day is what helps her establish the correct boundary.

Logic, Multiple Causes, and Differences of Degree

Once the child can separate fantasy and reality and separate logic from illogic, she progresses to multicausal thinking. Now she can give you several reasons for conditions and events: "It's cold outside because the sun isn't shining and because it's wintertime." "Arthur is sad because his father had to leave and also no one will play with him."

When your child can start giving you multiple reasons, her reality and her thinking ability become more complicated. This leads to indirect thinking, or triangular thinking. This skill is in play when a child can figure out that to win the Revolutionary War we had to enlist the help of France because that country was the enemy of England, who was our enemy. That is pretty sophisticated thinking. This skill can be acted out on the playground, too, when Eddie becomes friends with little Jeff by deliberately becoming friends with Jeff's friend. Eddie may have yearned to be friends with Jeff, but he became aware that Jeff didn't welcome his overtures. So Eddie's next move was to play ball with Billy, who is already Jeff's friend. Through Billy, he can play with Jeff, his original goal. This skill at triangular thinking skill applies to math, to understanding politics, and to negotiating the social world. It's a more advanced stage of logical thinking.

From there, we get into gray-area thinking. Now the child begins to figure out the degree to which things are true. For example, if a child is reading *The Adventures of Tom Sawyer* and you ask her why she likes Huck Finn more than Tom Sawyer, or vice versa, she may respond, "I like Huck Finn better because Huck is braver," "Huck is smarter," or "Huck is funnier." This demonstrates comparative thinking. The child is not simply saying, "I like Huck Finn because he's funny." She is actually comparing qualities inherent in the two characters.

For gray-area, differentiated thinking, a child must not only compare two things but also compare them in degrees. Similarly, we see it in a student who can not only name several reasons for the Civil War, such as slavery, states' rights, and economic factors, but also explore to what degree each played a role in the conflict.

This is sophisticated logic. Without this kind of thinking, a person is left with polarized, all-or-nothing thinking. We see children (and adults) who live in a black or white world where there are only good people or evil people, right answers or wrong answers. We're all familiar with that kind of rigid thinking. We see it in politics, we see it in religious cults, and we see it in misuses of science.

Children acquire this more sophisticated way of thinking by discussing their opinions and being asked nuanced questions: "What's more important to you: playing with that puzzle or coming on a hike?" Gray-area thinking breaks down into two components: *comparative* thinking, where you compare two things (such as why the first Harry Potter book was better than the others), and *differentiated* thinking, where you discuss the degrees to which A is better than B or why you like A more than B, or why one opinion is more persuasive than another. You can see these components in action on the playground when children designate a first-best friend, a second-best friend, and a third-best friend, and when they can tell you which personality or physical traits they like better than others in which person—and can quantify these shades of difference from day to day.

Logic and Self-Reflection

Finally, children can reach the ability to apply logic to an internal standard. This means developing the ability to evaluate your own thoughts and your own biases, and it usually comes into play in the teenage years. A child becomes able to look at her own writing, sports performance, math problems, or how she treated a friend. In the emotional area, this high-level thinking skill allows someone to say, "Boy, I really lost it today. I wonder why I got so mad? I don't usually do that." It helps an adolescent judge herself apart from the norms of a group: "The kids at school are sneaking off for cigarettes, but that's dumb. I don't want to take that chance"; or, "I'll see if I can get along with my friends in spite of not going along with their beer-drinking." A teenager's ability to evaluate himself, not to be swayed by the day-to-day world of peer relationships but to take a longer view of things, allows him to keep a steady course in a world of increasing temptation and risk.

How many adults truly have the capacity to judge themselves or their own biases? It's actually a rare commodity. It starts building in adolescence and represents a high level of logical and reflective thinking—but it is not easy to acquire. We can help our children evaluate themselves not simply by engaging them in opinion-oriented discussions ("What did you think about that movie?" "Is it fair to raise the age for a driver's license?") but also by asking them to judge their own work or behavior.

We don't often ask teenagers to grade their own essays and then compare that result with how the teacher grades it. A very interesting exercise is to have a child write an essay and then, a day or two later, grade and judge it herself. Was she tired that day? Did she do all the research needed? Then the teacher grades and judges it, and the child can compare the two analyses. She will then learn how well she judges herself. This ability is likely to grow with practice.

We are usually so busy telling children whether they've done a good or bad job that we rarely ask them to judge themselves. But we can give them criteria, let them set standards, and help them begin to become their own judges. Let them play the parental or teacher function so that they have an internal guide and can become their own mentors. This skill becomes more and more important for excelling in academic work, for getting along in society, and for operating in the complex political and economic world of adulthood. What more important skill can we give to teenagers as they enter that world?

ENCOURAGING LOGIC AND
REFLECTIVE THINKING

We all want our children to be clear-headed individuals who can observe objective facts in a way that helps them operate in the real world. We don't want their emotions to skew their perception of what is real, yet neither do we want to raise brilliant, icy robots.

If you watch your baby closely, you'll see the seeds of logical thinking budding out of her emotional connection with you in the very first months of life. When your nursing three- or four-month-old pulls her mouth away from her bottle so that she can flash you a loopy grin, she is immediately rewarded by your heartwarming smile. She's learning that she has an impact on the world, that what she does will cause a predictable response.

Six months later, she'll be enlisting more of her senses and newfound motor skills to drum up exciting responses. When she chortles in delight as she scuttles away from you, looking expectantly over her shoulder, you'll chuckle right back at her. During this first year of life, parents do more than simply respond to a baby's overtures; they woo her with gestures and words that keep her coming back for more. When she spies a new teddy bear in the box at your feet, for example, you are likely to nod toward the box, inviting her to pick up the new toy. When she clutches the bear, you might open your arms wide, beckon to her, and see whether she'll give the toy back to you. Each time you challenge her to respond to you, you're helping her to experience the world as a purposeful, logical place.

When a child is two or so, you'll notice that she's beginning to use ideas and even a few words to express her desires and to solve problems. When the two of you play hide-and-seek and you run into the next room and crouch behind the sofa, you'll observe her entering the room and yanking back a curtain or peeking under the card table. She's got an idea, a mental picture, of those places where you've popped up when you played together earlier, and she's using those pictures logically to help her solve the puzzle at hand.

When she's four years old and a word master, you can enjoy reality-based conversations. This is a time when more is better, and only non sequiturs should be avoided. Children of this age are often distractible and get a little lost in the ideas that flood their minds. They'll need your help in making logical sense.

Let's say you've just finished watching a fantasy video with your child one Saturday afternoon and decide that it's time for less sedentary fun. As the two of you walk hand in hand toward the backyard, you're likely to turn to her and ask, "Well now, what shall we play?" She may start mumbling: "Aladdin's carpet can't really fly; it's just pretend." She's finding it hard to shake off the world of fantasy she's been immersed in for the past ninety minutes and is in need of your assistance to focus on the present.

You can help her conversations make sense by catching her eye and saying, "You're right, but I was asking what games you'd like to play with me. What shall we do next?" You can then give her some reality-based choices: "How about the swing? Or would you rather plant some more carrot seeds? Maybe you want to finish building the bird house." When she jubilantly cries out, "Yes, let's build it and the birds can fly there on their magic carpet!" you can be assured that you've helped her form a plan of action based on her desires, yet not remain lost in the make-believe world.

Now that she's back in the game and making sense, it's clear that she wants to continue exploring the theme of Aladdin's magic carpet. Ask her to tell you why riding on a carpet is more exciting than riding in the car. When she starts to reel off a number of reasons why carpet rides are superior—"Because you get to go above the trees and you don't have to buy gas and you don't need a driving license"—she's showing you that her logical thinking is becoming more refined.

One day when she's nine and you're at the bicycle shop trying to decide which bike to buy, you'll have one of many opportunities to facilitate her new ability to handle subtle, gray-area thinking. Your daughter may know that she wants a 10-speed bike, but she finds it hard to make a decision because there are so many models. Ask her to make a checklist of all the bells and whistles she really wants. Ask lots of questions to help her zero in on those features she'd like to find in a bike. You can then have her rank the features in order of importance.

When your daughter takes a second look at the bikes that have caught her eye and figures out which one matches her wishlist most closely, she's showing you that with your help she can look at all the bikes and make logical comparisons (one particular 10-speed model wasn't her favorite color but was a little less expensive, had gears that were easy to shift, and was equipped with lights that flashed in the dark). The "How Many Reasons" game she played with you during her nursery school days has morphed into a "Rank Your Reasons" exercise based on her growing ability to think logically in many areas.

Sometime as early as age nine or ten and as late as the mid-teens, a child will be capable of assessing her own logic. That's a very sophisticated level of thinking because she must not only produce the logical creation (the essay, the excuse about why her homework was late, a "pro" argument in debate class) but also stand back and dispassionately, logically, decide just how clear her thinking was.

Parents can help their child do this by asking simple questions—"How well do you think you made your case?"—in a nonthreatening way. They can also stage friendly dinner-table debates and designate a judge who remains above the fray. (The term of office lasts for one debate only and everybody gets a chance to don the robes.) Each debater presents three arguments in support of her point of view and then explains which one of the points is the most compelling—an exercise in logical analysis and self-evaluation. Next, the judge weighs in on which of the participants' "top" arguments was the most logically persuasive and whether she agrees with each debater's evaluation of the relative strength of his or her arguments.

Self-evaluation is daunting at any age. But the more you can encourage your teen not simply to embrace success but to recognize and logically assess failure, the less likely it is that she'll become immobilized by despondency or shame. Great kids aren't defensive blowhards. They're nuanced, logical thinkers who see the world through realistic eyes.

Helping Your Baby Make Sense of the World

1. Tune into your baby, responding to her cues and challenging her to respond to you. Let her know that what she does makes an impact on the world.
2. Make room for many long conversations with her.
3. Challenge her to "make sense" when her responses to you are nonsensical.
4. Ask her for more than one reason for things, more than one way of looking at an issue.
5. Help her compare her preferences in books, movies, sports.
6. In discussing opinions, ask for degrees, such as which attribute is more important and by how much.
7. Let her judge her own behavior, her arguments, her schoolwork. Give her practice in self-evaluation, but be sure it is constructive and that she is not incapacitated by failures.

When our children move into the late teenage years and the young adult years, their ability for critical thinking is challenged by a broader range of experiences. As these adolescents experience all the biological changes, more intimate relationships, changing friendships, stiff competition in high school and in college admission, will their self-reflective skills remain intact? Can they maintain these skills as they leave their nuclear families and move to college dorms and then on to jobs? Will they be able to take care of themselves and refine their internal sets of values? Can they do this amidst the intense emotional ups and downs these years? Will their abilities to reflect on themselves hold strong when they have their own children and revisit the stages of development with them? If you have been with them, questioning them and encouraging them through the journey

I've just described, chances are good that they will. As we empathetically understand our own children's development and broaden their perspectives on the world to include individuals in other cultures, their sense of reality and capacity for logical reflection ripens and deepens.

Meanwhile, we as parents face new perspectives on the cycles of life. We no longer see life as infinite and ourselves as omnipotent. But as we and our children engage in broadening and deepening experiences, including the contemplation of the end of our lives, certain strengthened values and broader thinking allow us each to achieve a kind of peace with our lives, ourselves, and those we love. The need for self-reflection never ends while we are alive and kicking. As we make better and better sense of our world, we help our children reflect logically on theirs.

10

Moral Integrity
A Matter of the Heart

·····················

Michael, a college freshman, was faced with his first examination in a difficult geology course. He had studied hard and, to his relief, he knew most of the answers. At the end of the three-hour exam, he closed his blue book with a sigh of satisfaction. Only then did he notice a printed form on the front of the booklet. It said: "I have neither given nor received aid on this examination," and it had a space for signing his name and adding the date.

Now, this young man had attended a Quaker school—although he was not a member of the Society of Friends—and all his exams in high school had been given on the honor system. There were no proctors prowling the aisles of his high school exam rooms as there were here at college.

Both at home and at school, Michael had had a lot of experience talking with adults. So when he handed in the test, he joked with the professor:

"You know, I'm happy to tell you that I did not give or receive help on this exam. But I've never had to sign a pledge about it before."

"We've had that pledge for years," the professor said. "It's no big deal."

"But if I had cheated, what would prevent me from cheating some more and signing this pledge? Seriously, I believe that 'trust' has to grow from getting to know each other. You'll get to know my work over time," Michael couldn't resist replying.

The professor recognized that although Michael was taking a lighthearted approach, he was arguing a strongly held principle; he decided to accept the freshman's verbal affirmation that he had not cheated on the geology exam. He also agreed with Michael's "serious" argument.

Why did Michael feel confident enough about his own integrity to chaff the professor about the honor pledge? Who and what had calibrated his inner moral compass? As with all the traits that create a great kid, a sense of integrity is instilled early in the interactions and rituals of a family.

THE ROOTS OF INTEGRITY

Depending on the child and his family, a sense of ethics and morality will be embedded in a variety of worldviews and religious and cultural beliefs. Many value systems, regardless of their origins, have much in common in the ways they guide people to work responsibly together in groups and help family members to support one another compassionately. The key for parents is to understand how their children absorb the ethics,

morality, and values of the family and its religion and culture—
and ultimately to embrace, adapt, or reject them.

Many people think of values, ideals, ethics, and morality as
guideposts that help them figure out right from wrong. But is
the ability to categorize what is right and wrong, what will be
punished and what won't be punished, really at the heart of
ethics and morality? For a great kid, and a great adult, the heart
of morality is the ability to *care* about what is right and wrong.
College freshman Michael not only knew that cheating on a test
is wrong and can have unpleasant consequences but also cared
enough about his own work and his own standards not even to
consider cheating. He understands that cheating makes exams
meaningless because it diminishes not only the cheater's learning but everyone else's as well.

It's quite possible to be able to distinguish right and wrong but
not care about doing the right thing. A child on the playground
can know it's right to be nice to another child but wrong to steal
his ball or to hit and push him: "Yes, I know it's wrong and I
know I'll be punished if I get caught," he may cavalierly tell himself, "but no one is around to watch me. I'm going to push Stevie
because he grabbed the first place in line when we went out to
recess." When the opportunity to shove Stevie without getting
caught comes along, there is no little angel on this child's shoulder telling him not to do it.

But as we see in many middle and high schools now, it's not
just simply pushing that goes on in playing fields and in the
hallways. A student may come in with a weapon and seriously
injure or hurt another classmate who "did something to me" or
"didn't give me respect." And it's not just among teenagers that
this happens; we are seeing it occur at younger and younger
ages. Many of these children know the difference between right

and wrong in an intellectual sense. After the fact, they can say to you: "I was wrong to do it, I know it's not what you're supposed to do." They can even recite the punishments that face them. They understand consequences, they understand that they will be punished for cheating on a test or that they could go to jail for hurting someone. Yet they choose to do it anyway. They may think they can get away with it, but what is missing is that they don't care.

Early in this book is a chapter on one of the most important traits that characterizes a great kid: the quality of empathy, of being able to care about another person and to recognize the validity of his feelings. I want to focus now on integrity, because it, too, is a crucial quality that not only makes for great kids, but also helps sustain civilization and create a world in which people can live together in peace. These two qualities might be considered bookends that hold upright the other qualities possessed by great kids.

Three key elements have to be in place to develop morality and a sense of ethics. You need to be able to distinguish right from wrong, and you need to be able to understand the values that underpin your culture and society. But, most important, you have to care. *Morality is a matter of the heart, a matter of caring, not just of knowing the difference between right and wrong.* In the words of the psychiatrist Robert Coles, "A well-developed conscience does not translate, necessarily, into a morally courageous life."

Lots of adults struggle with morality and integrity. Everyday we read in the newspapers that people in the business community are "cheating" in the way they manipulate their business dealings. Some have finally gone to jail for their violations. Others have been ostracized publicly. We see political leaders having difficulties with their "moral and ethical" behavior. We observe individuals preach the highest levels of ethical behavior and then in their private lives breach these very same principles.

Of course, all of us will "cheat" a little around the edges from time to time. Little children want to get an extra point in a game or sneak an extra brownie off the platter. And there are few adults who haven't pocketed a dollar bill they've found lying on the sidewalk. But these little incursions, these minor human frailties, are very different from major lapses in the fundamental moral and ethical codes that hold societies together. To find out how moral integrity develops, as with so many other questions about raising great kids, we need to go back to the beginning.

Learning to Care

I watched a new grandmother holding her three-week-old grandson, Noah, the other day. She was seated in the middle of a row of chairs before a school performance began, with other families ahead of and behind her. As she held the tiny red-faced baby lolling on her shoulder, other people—including strangers—stopped to greet her as they passed by.

"What a lovely baby," "Is it a boy?" "He looks so peaceful," they commented. They reached out and patted his tiny hands and stroked his back. The little boy was not only shored up by his grandma's shoulder but surrounded by the love and welcome of his community. As he grows up, these other adults will continue to play a role in making him feel loved and in introducing him to the norms of his world—one of the first being the progressive preschool his older sister attends. Even in these very first encounters, Noah is learning about caring.

Caring starts in the early months, as a baby has that first, loving relationship with the people who take care of him. If that relationship is characterized by warmth, love, and involvement, if there is more pleasure and more trust than there is pain, disruption, or disorganization, then we have the beginnings of a baby who will buy into the human race. He will feel part of several relationships that are pleasurable and enjoyable. Bit by bit, those who care for this little boy are finding their way into his heart.

In thirty years of research and clinical observations, I have seen that *this* wonderful process can happen every time. Every child—and I mean every child, not 99 percent of children—has a reachable heart. I have yet to meet a baby who could not be wooed into a caring relationship, regardless of his challenges and special needs. And don't try to talk to me about "bad seed" kids; I've never met one.

The key with children of every level of ability is to work around their individual style of taking in the world. Each child has a different way of reacting to touch or sound, of figuring out sounds and words, of planning actions, and of relating to others. We reach children by joining them in their world and then pulling them into ours. We do it by tailoring our approach to the child. For the child who is sensitive to sound, we are especially soothing and soft. For children who need more energy, we enthusiastically pull them in. With every child, we help them become part of a relationship. In this way, children grow up caring about other people. They become loving people, no matter what challenges they may face.

Establishing a relationship is what Noah's grandmother was up to as she cradled and cooed to the little bundle in her arms. And that is what you can do by establishing a relationship with your own miraculous baby. For your baby, falling in love with the rest of the human race establishes the foundation for caring he will stand on all his life.

At each developmental level, your child learns from the responses of his caregivers. When he sees that one set of responses brings a warm smile and "You're the best baby in the world," but another set makes Mommy's head shake "No-no," her voice low-pitched and stern, he learns to shape his behavior accordingly. The pleasure he gets from a smile and a warm cuddle is the beginning of learning right from wrong.

Being Mean, Being Nice

As your child progresses to the next level, he is not only learning about basic right and wrong—what gets him in trouble and what doesn't—but also about the subtleties of right and wrong. While playing in the sandbox, he learns the difference between a gentle pat, which is friendly and loving, and an angry push that knocks someone down and makes him cry. Of course, toddlers will still do the latter, sometimes as a test of their own power, but even as they do it they are learning the differences in right and wrong because of how the other person's reactions make them feel.

I recently saw a toddler extend his ratty, but beloved, teddy bear to a crying child on the playground as a temporary comfort. He stood by nervously as the other child quieted down, and he looked immensely relieved when he got his teddy back. But he had made the gesture and seemed to understand and be happy that it worked.

At this stage, children don't need to understand the abstract idea we call "altruism" to do something kind. They don't necessarily have a set of articulated ideas: "I want to be nice to Mommy because it will make her feel good." But they are beginning to learn that if Mommy looks sad and they cuddle up in her lap and give her a big hug and a kiss, Mommy will give a big smile and both of them will feel better.

Altruistic behavior in children by eighteen months of life has been observed not only by us but by many other researchers. These toddlers' behavior is not accompanied by a sophisticated understanding of why they're being kind. Rather, it operates at the level of an intuitive emotional response of wanting to make a parent happy or wanting to make a friend feel better after he falls and hurts his knee. Before words, the kind response is understood and practiced through gestures and expressions.

As altruism develops, so does its less attractive twin, cruelty. If you spend much time on the playground, you will see small children who have become more organized in their aggression. They are more skillful at hurting people, at teasing, at pinching, at biting, at doing mean things. You might even note toddlers beginning to exclude other peers and forming little toddler "in" groups. You don't have to wait for the teenage years to see that dynamic at work.

"Bozo was bad!": Learning Morality Through Imaginative Play

In the third year of life, as children engage in pretend play and use their ideas creatively, we begin to see them developing attitudes in the world of ideas, not just in behaviors, about what's good and what's bad. They imagine evil villains stealing away the princess, and then they conjure up "good guys" with magical powers to save her.

From about age two through ages four or five, this creative pretending burgeons and involves intense experimentation with good and evil and noble and wicked. If you join your children in their shared imaginative world, you can help them develop a more subtle understanding of these themes. With the child who just plays by himself, the same theme may get a little repetitive.

But if you are playing with your son, you can ask, "Why is Froggy so good and Bozo so bad? What did they do?"—in essence you are deepening the soap opera. Your involvement can help the characters develop. "Why are you attacking me, Bozo? What did I do to you?" As the plot of imaginative play thickens, children can explore ideas of good and evil.

Each culture and each religion and each family has its own take on right and wrong and good and bad. The key to imparting your own values to your child is *not* to restrict the themes of your shared pretend play but instead to join in and follow his lead. You can then show him the values you want by playing them out in the role and actions of the character you've assumed. He may fight them at first, but he'll learn about them, and may embrace them eventually. This works much, much better than trying to be the boss of games yourself. Life is too complicated for rigid rules and standards. If you simply tell your child what his character should and should not do, he's likely to rebel and behave contrarily. You need to help your child develop subtle judgments, and that happens through the dialogues that go on in imaginative play.

Empathy and Morality

As children learn to be logical, to connect their ideas together and ask "why" questions, parents have a great opportunity not only to explore values and goals but to model ideals and a sense of morality. Now you can ask a child, "Why are you so angry?" or "Why did you hit Brian?" or "Why did you steal that cookie?" If you empathize with the child and understand him, you are teaching a critical value. The child learns empathy and caring not from what you tell him to do but from what he experiences with you. So if you listen respectfully to the child even when he is hostile and angry and mean, it softens his feeling and keeps his anger from existing in one world and his caring in another.

We see far too many people who can be caring with the left hand and enraged and angry with the right, as if the left and right hands don't know each other. We say, "How could so-and-so go to a religious service over the weekend and express such empathy and compassion, and then turn around and be so mean-spirited and aggressive during the week?" Well, individuals like that compartmentalize their worlds. We need more people—more great kids and great adults—whose whole beings work in a concerted way.

When you show a caring understanding to a child, even when he is feeling angry and mean, and you help him explain the basis of his feelings, he will learn to connect your caring with his anger. The only way to learn empathy is to be treated with empathy.

This does not mean that you don't punish or set up sanctions with your four-year-old when he crosses the line, when he hits his sister or bites a friend. Not at all. You establish appropriate limits and consequences for the child's actions, as well as exhibit empathy and understanding for why he did it.

You can do this in steps:

- Help the child calm down when he is upset: "I can't understand you when you are screaming."
- Once he is calm, talk about the why and how of what he did and the feelings behind it: "Why did you push over Alex's bike? Were you angry with him?"
- Institute appropriate consequences, sanctions, or limits, depending on what he did. If he just yelled and screamed, he didn't cross the line and needs only to calm down. But if he hit or bit, not in self-defense but in anger, there may be an appropriate sanction. You should have talked about

these sanctions with him in advance so that he knows what happens when he misbehaves. But keep in mind that you want him to see you as a kindly policeman who is interested in understanding him and helping him to avoid doing it again, as opposed to a furious policeman who is going to banish him without caring how he feels.

When you set limits in this way you are modeling your values. You will be raising a child who can control himself, who internalizes limits, who wants to follow your guidelines, and who has compassion for himself and for others. He will want to do better. He will want to please you and eventually please himself.

Complicating the Equation

The move to the next stage of development, more subtle and refined ideas of right and wrong, reminds me of one of those tic-tac-toe boards that is set up on three levels, like the scaffolding of a three-story building. Suddenly a simple game becomes more complex as it operates in more than one dimension. Your child's intellectual and emotional life, and his development, is becoming multilayered as well.

Now your child learns not only to think logically but also to look for many reasons for right and wrong and many different degrees of each: "Was Deirdre right to put Alec out of the game for cheating?" "How bad is it to take someone's turn, if you have a really good idea?"

As a child masters these new complicated ways of thinking, you can have richer and deeper—and subtler—discussions with him. He may ask, "What do I do when Max is a bully? Do I tell the teacher? If I tell the teacher, the kids are going to call me a sissy. If I hit Max, I'll get in trouble. What's the answer?"

Well, that's not such a simple question. That situation requires a big discussion. With the child who has moved into gray-area thinking, we can be a good sideline coach and say, "Well, what do you think? Let's reason this out together. How would you feel if you (A) went to the teacher and the kids teased you about it? How would you feel if (B) you pushed back but then got in trouble for it? How would you feel if (C) you asserted yourself with just a loud voice but not with pushing so you wouldn't get into trouble? Or how would you feel if (D) you just avoided those kids and hung out with other kids you like or new friends? What would feel best? What might happen? How would they feel?"

There is no one straightforward answer here, as much as you might wish for one. Adults don't have easy answers when these questions arise in their own peer groups, either. But if you and your child take the time to reason it through, you're giving him far more than a solution to a problem that popped up on the playground that day. You're teaching him to think about social relationships and to weigh the different moral and ethical issues involved in each decision. You are helping him learn ways to solve future problems. When life becomes complicated, we must learn to think on our feet. That's the ultimate goal: a child who has instilled within himself the capacity for reflective, moral, and ethical thinking.

The Courage of One's Own Convictions

At the next level, from about ages ten to fourteen, your child will begin to create his own internal standards and values. These will stand him in good stead as he moves through the shifting sands of school and peer and home life. During these years, a child can lay down a bedrock sense of "good and bad."

This is also the time when your child's spirituality is evolving toward something closer to its adult form. This inner sense of depth and meaning may be embodied in a set of religious beliefs, in cultural or family values, or in the child's own amalgamation of all these based on his experience. Along with the sense of right and wrong, these beliefs can become the moral compass mentioned before. It gives the child the perspective and strength to say, for example, "Those football players were being mean to that kid. I should have tried to get them to stop." In other words, he develops an inner voice that is separate from the moment-to-moment clamor coming from his peer group. This inner voice can hold itself together and survive even temporary shifts in feelings.

In earlier eras, and often today, those inner standards constituted what was called "character." Robert Coles, who interviewed children and adolescents all over the country for his book *The Moral Life of Children,* points out that for adolescents character is not a rigid or categorical trait: "For them, character is not a possession, but something one searches for; a quality of mind and heart one struggles for, at times with a bit more success than at others."

Each time your child gets angry or panicky or sad or embarrassed or frustrated, he has a chance to become better able to maintain a set of personal values, an inner voice against which he can compare the feeling of the moment: "I really shouldn't throw that tennis ball over the high wall so the other kids can't use it. It's not fair, and it's mean—but it sure is tempting!"

That kind of reasoning doesn't occur in the minds of most six- or seven-year-olds. They are not yet capable of it. Although fourteen-year-olds are capable of such reasoning, many don't embrace it quite yet; if they do, they are inconsistent. But it is ultimately that kind of reasoning that enables one to be a moral and ethical person.

As youngsters reach that level of reasoning in which they can live in two worlds at once—the world of internal values, which is stable, and the world of moment-to-moment changes in feelings and experiences and challenges—they learn to keep comparing the two. When they are able to do that, they can shape an inner sense of self of which they are proud.

RAISING A MORAL CHILD

No righteous finger wagging or batch of rote Sunday school lessons can ensure that your child will care about doing the "right" thing. He'll learn about ethics and morality not from what you tell him but from how you treat him.

In the earliest weeks and months of life, as you cuddled your baby, you may have observed that by holding him close to your breast he was comforted by the warmth of your skin and the steady, reassuring rhythm of your beating heart. Or perhaps you noticed that lowering the shades in his bedroom seemed to relax him enough so that he could solemnly exchange wide-eyed stares with you.

These little comforting touches let your child feel cared-for in a profound way. When you promptly attend to his physical needs by feeding him when he cries with hunger, or rubbing his back when a tummy ache causes him to stiffen his little legs in pain, he experiences the emotional balm of your smiles and the tenderness in handling him. Over time and with your help, he'll come not only to expect caring from others but also to extend it to others because he knows how good it feels.

In years of practice, I've sorrowfully seen just how devastating it can be when youngsters don't receive a foundation of appropriate caring, love, and respect. Children who have been treated harshly and sadistically have a strong tendency to want to be harsh and sadistic back. When a parent, caregiver, or other authority figure is around, they may inhibit that tendency and appear to be "good citizens"; but when they're away from authority figures, the early harshness or indifference they endured often emerges in irresponsible or cruel behavior to other children and animals. This behavior is often combined with sadness and depression.

For these children, "being good" simply becomes a means to an end; they toe the line only because it brings them benefits. Having never been given the opportunity to internalize the sweet pleasure of being loved and cared for, they can have no intuitive feeling that caring for and helping others simply feels good.

At eight to eighteen months, the gesturing that gets merrily under way teaches your child that the world is a logical place where his nods, shouts of glee, tugs on your sleeve and beseeching glances are met with encouraging responses. He also begins to see himself as separate from you and a worthy, beloved playmate. This play also provides him with early lessons in right and wrong. When he crosses a behavioral line, your melodramatic frowns, firm gripping of his hands, sad sighs, and vigorous head shaking present him with a visible picture that he's done something wrong.

During the toddler years, children want concrete rules: It's bad to hit, it's nice to share. As you sit on the floor and join your two-and-a-half-year-old in a rollicking dinosaur party or follow your three-year-old's lead when his toy firemen become avenging super heroes, it's not unlikely that your child will get overexcited and slip into "bad" behavior in which he hurts himself or others or breaks a toy or two.

That's when he'll need the reliable limit setting that only you or another loving caretaker can provide. When he has a meltdown because things haven't gone his way, or you've reined him in when he deliberately kicks the toys in all directions, you'll impose the calming structure he so obviously needs.

Scaring your child with enraged looks and threats doesn't produce ethical or moral values; setting firm, gentle, persistent limits, coupled with respect and empathy, does. So when he's working up to a tantrum, first try calming him by empathetically commenting on his frustration in a soothing voice; next, subtly attempt to shift his attention to a quieter, yet pleasurable, activity. Even when you don't succeed in immediately helping him regain his cool, he senses that you're in there with him, that you're on his side. By being treated with respect, your child will be less defensive when you do have to impose a sanction.

If he should lash out violently when his little brother takes his favorite puppet, or transgresses in some other way, your first order of business might well be to take him aside and help him calm down. When he's breathing a little more quietly, you can take on a "good cop" role and talk to him about why his bad behavior can't continue, even though you understand that he's angry. Such conversations are best conducted away from the scene of the crime so that your child won't be distracted from your soothing by the sight of the source of his anger or frustration.

Next, you'll talk to him about why he's going to need some limits set on his behavior, and what those limits will be. Then reassure him that all will be well when the punishment is over. Don't stifle his unhappy or angry words, but help him rephrase them in ways that are less energized. Listen with respect, but point out consequences that arise out of his behavior that he surely didn't consider. When he finally relinquishes that last shuddering sigh, and all his pent-up frustration with it, try to talk soothingly about how he could better handle his angry feelings the next time he experiences them. Finally, let him know that you, too, have experienced similar feelings, and you know how hard it is not to act "bad" sometimes. Your empathy will calm and reassure him, and it will allow him to save a little face, too.

Isolating him, sending him to his room to brood by himself, usually won't help him regain control. That kind of penalty has a mean quality to it that disrupts any empathetic warmth you may have reestablished with your child. Have him sit quietly on a chair near you for a while instead, not allowed to play a favorite game for a designated period, or make amends by companionably doing some chores alongside you. This kind of limit setting is both respectful and comforting. He'll internalize these feelings and will want to recapture them in the future.

As your schoolchild gradually becomes aware that things are not fair all the time, he'll also be increasingly thrown into ambiguous situations where he has to make decisions based on what seems to be the most fair, or ethical, or moral choice he can possibly make. Until he's nine or so, concrete rules about what's right and what's wrong have served him pretty well. You've sheltered him from many of the moral ambiguities and questions-with-no-easy-answers that await him out in the big world, but now that he's joining groups and venturing out on his own, he's confronting many more moral puzzles.

Maxims such as "It's bad to push and shove" and "It's nice to share" won't supply him with ready guidance when he's facing down three fierce defenders trying to block his way to the soccer goal. He certainly won't be sharing the ball with the other team, so the old rules you've instilled in him about sharing with others won't work in this new context.

The kind of ambiguous situation that will face adolescents was explored by a psychologist named Lawrence Kolberg, who studied the different levels of thinking involved in making moral judgments: "Suppose you're an adult and your grandmother is ill and needs medicine immediately or she won't survive the night. The drugstore in town is the only place where you can get the medicine, but it's closed. Do you break in and steal the lifesaving medicine or do you follow the rules?"

As you talk with your teenager about the complex ethical problems that are evident in this example, you'll be helping him shoulder responsibility for making tough decisions when he's on his own. Does he think that saving his grandmother's life is a moral imperative that entitles him to break the law? What if his grandmother wasn't a very nice person? Do the ends always justify the means when a human life is at stake? Suppose the pharmacist was working late and was so frightened by the sounds of an intruder that he had a heart attack and died. How would he feel about his actions then? Such philosophical musings will help your high school child become a logical, subtle thinker, and they will also enable him to think increasingly creatively in the realm of right and wrong.

Usually, the dilemmas faced by a teenager are not such life-or-death ones, but emotionally they can still matter a great deal. Let's say Lottie has two really good friends and she can't be with both of them on the last night before each takes off for summer vacation. How does she handle the situation in a way that won't hurt one of her friends' feelings?

A parent can reassure Lottie by empathetically acknowledging that she really is in a delicate situation, one that most adults wouldn't know how to handle very well, either. They might explore whether there's room for telling a small white lie to one of the girls to spare her feelings. Yet you've always emphasized the importance of being a straight-shooter and of telling the truth. Should she avoid the situation by doing something with her family instead of making plans with one of her friends? Which is the more ethical decision for Lottie to make?

Encouraging Morality

1. Help a child calm down when he is upset.
2. Ask him how he is feeling and why.
3. Treat a child of any age with empathy and respect; he learns from the behavior you model rather than from your words.
4. Set firm, but gentle and proportionate, limits.
5. Initiate lots of "what if" discussions in advance of problematic situations that inevitably arise during early adolescence and the teen years.
6. Tell your child about moral dilemmas you've experienced, actions you've regretted, inspiring mentors you've known, and the religious or ethical traditions in your family history.

There will be no easy answers for your young adult to take solace in as he struggles with these kinds of complex moral and ethical questions. But by engaging him in Socratic debate, by asking him where, when, why, how, and to-what-degree questions rather than making solemn declarations about doing the right thing, you'll be providing him with the kind of practice he needs to think with subtlety in the years ahead and the kind of intellectual rigor that all great kids possess.

Parents who encourage this self-reflection in themselves and their children have an effect on the larger society. They raise children who are less apt to hurt people or to be mean-spirited and destroy things. Such inner values help bind the larger global community and care for the planet itself.

As adolescents move toward adulthood, they become able to project themselves mentally into the future and integrate it with the past and the present. They are also better able to see another's point of view, to walk in someone else's shoes for a while. These new insights and empathy are honed as they move into more intimate connections, more long-term commitments. As adolescents head off to college and the workplace and then prepare to raise families of their own, they will carry the values they learned with you onward. You will be within them, in the integrity and values you shaped together along the paths from infancy to adolescence, through all those conversations, arguments, debates, all that loving concern.

Finally, if you are lucky, you will have the wonderful opportunity to teach those same values of understanding and caring to your children's children, to new generations. This is the way civilizations and cultures continue. And it takes great kids to build them.

Bibliography

······················

Brazelton, T. Berry. *Touchpoints Birth to Three*. Cambridge, MA: Da Capo Press, 2006.

Coles, R. *The Moral Life of Children*. Boston: Houghton Mifflin, 1986.

Erikson, Erik. *Childhood and Society*. New York: W. W. Norton, 1950, 1963.

Fraiberg, Selma. *The Magic Years*. New York: Charles Scribner's Sons, 1959.

Greenspan, Stanley I. *Building Healthy Minds*. Cambridge, MA: Da Capo Press, 1999.

————. *The Growth of the Mind*. Cambridge, MA: Da Capo Press, 1997.

Greenspan, Stanley I., and Stuart Shanker. *The First Idea*. Cambridge, MA: Da Capo Press, 2004.

Handley, Helen, and Andrea Samuelson, eds. *The Child*. New York: Penguin Books, 1990.

Holt, John. *How Children Learn*. Cambridge, MA: Da Capo Press, 1983.

Kagan, Jerome. *The Nature of the Child*. New York: Basic Books, 1984.

Kohlberg, Lawrence. *The Philosophy of Moral Development*. New York: Harper and Row, 1981.

Langer, Ellen. *Mindfulness*. Cambridge, MA: Da Capo Press, 1989.

Papert, Seymour. *Mindstorms*. New York: Basic Books, 1993.

Photography Credits

....

Index

....

About the Author

. . . .

Stanley I. Greenspan, M.D., is Clinical Professor of Psychiatry
and Pediatrics at George Washington University Medical School
and Chairman of the Interdisciplinary Council on Developmental and Learning Disorders. He is the world's foremost authority
on clinical work with infants and young children who have developmental and emotional problems, and his work is the basis for
regional networks for which he guides their care. He is the found-
ing president of Zero to Three: The National Center for Infants,
Toddlers and Families, past director of the NIMH Mental Health
Study Center and the Clinical Infant Development Program, and
is a supervising child psychoanalyst at the Washington Psychoana-
lytic Institute. He is the recipient of many national and interna-
tional awards, including the American Psychiatric Association's
highest honor for child psychiatry research, as well as the Sigour-
ney Prize for Outstanding Contributions to Psychoanalysis.
Dr. Greenspan is the author of more than a hundred scholarly
articles and chapters and the author or editor of more than forty
books (translated into more than a dozen languages), including
Engaging Autism: Using the Floortime Approach to Helping Children

Relate, Communicate, and Think (coauthored with Serena Wieder, Ph.D.); *The First Idea: How Symbols, Language, and Intelligence Evolved in Early Primates and Humans* (coauthored with Stuart G. Shanker, Ph.D.); *The Growth of the Mind, Building Healthy Minds, The Challenging Child, The Child with Special Needs* (coauthored with Serena Wieder, Ph.D.), *Infancy and Early Childhood, Developmentally-Based Psychotherapy,* and *The Irreducible Needs of Children* (coauthored with T. Berry Brazelton, M.D.). His research has been featured in all the major media, including *Newsweek, Time,* the *Washington Post,* the *New York Times,* ABC, NBC, and CBS news broadcasts, and was the subject of a PBS NOVA documentary, *Life's First Feelings.*